SKIN
IN THE
GAME

RICK LAWRENCE

SKIN IN THE GAME

LIVING
AN EPIC
JESUS-CENTERED
LIFE

Kregel
Publications

To every follower of Jesus who is, right now, offering their skin in the game to help set captives free.

CONTENTS

Acknowledgments   / 9
Introduction   / 11

Chapter 1 | Will You Face Your Shame?   / 19
Chapter 2 | Will You Receive Grace?   / 35
Chapter 3 | Will You Embrace Your True Identity?   / 49
Chapter 4 | Will You Own What You Want?   / 67
Chapter 5 | Will You Confront Your Fears?   / 79
Chapter 6 | Will You Risk?   / 93
Chapter 7 | Will You Wait, Even When All Hope Is Lost?   / 103
Chapter 8 | Will You Make Jesus Your First and Last Resort?   / 117

Epilogue   / 135
Notes   / 139

ACKNOWLEDGMENTS

Talk to any author who also has a family, and they will tell you they are most indebted to those closest to them—the people who make the most visceral sacrifices to make it possible to write. So thank you to Bev, my wife, who not only inspires me and feeds my soul but also makes it possible for me to write these words. And thank you to my daughters, Lucy and Emma, for valuing who I am above what I do for you and for reminding me of the primacy of *home* in my life.

Thank you to Bev, Tom Melton, and Brad Behan for reading this manuscript at various stages of "work in progress," then offering me your insights, beefs, and raves.

I'm grateful, also, for the mentors in my life who have fueled my own pursuit of Jesus. Tom Melton and Bob Krulish are chief among them. Thanks as well to the "accidental mentors," living and dead, who have profoundly impacted me—C. S. Lewis, George MacDonald, G. K. Chesterton, C. H. Spurgeon, Hannah Hurnard, Walter Wangerin, Phillip Yancey, Edwin Friedman, Eugene Peterson, Dallas Willard, Tim Keller, John Ortberg, and John Eldredge. These people represent the little streams that flow into the Mississippi of my life, and I would have no "current" without them.

Thank you to the Mount St. Francis retreat center, the Krump family, and a host of scattered Starbucks for offering me refuge for writing.

Thank you to Greg Johnson for shepherding my trajectory as an author.

And thank you to Dennis Hillman, Steve Barclift, Noelle Pedersen, Leah Mastee, and Bob Hartig at Kregel for giving me the chance to publish this work and for working hard to make it better.

INTRODUCTION

The legend goes something like this . . .

In the late 1960s, the now-iconic investor Warren Buffet pried seed money for his very first stock fund from eleven doctors who'd agreed to kick in $105,000. Then, in an act of metaphoric chutzpah, Buffet added one hundred dollars of his own money to the kitty. No one knows exactly when the phrase "skin in the game" entered the American vernacular, but many pinned it on Buffet's experiment in financial poetry.[1] The now ubiquitous phrase captures the essence of an investment of heart and courage and risk, not the mere investment of money.

The idea is simple: You have no business asking others to trust you with their money if you're not willing to put your own resources at risk. If you have no "skin in the game," no stake of vulnerability, then your engagement is distant and rhetorical rather than personal and visceral. We might play fast and loose with others' resources but not with our own. Put another way, it's one thing to *work for* an entrepreneur; it's quite another to *be* the entrepreneur. The first involves little personal investment; the second demands our heart, our time, our sacrifice, our commitment—some real "skin."

When Araunah, the rich owner of a well-known threshing floor in Israel, offered King David not only his business but all the tools of his trade as well, so that David could build an altar to God, the King refused: "No, but I will surely buy it from you for a price, for I will not offer burnt offerings to the LORD my God which cost me nothing" (2 Sam. 24:24). David insisted on having his skin in the game—because a sacrifice that requires no sacrifice simply isn't a sacrifice.

Author and poet Henry David Thoreau wrote that "the mass of men lead lives of quiet desperation."[2] He was describing people who've chosen, with an inexorable bent toward pragmatism, to repeatedly step back from the precipice of risk. *They stubbornly resist putting their skin in the game.*

It's not hard to understand why. Life in a world decimated and twisted by sin can be punishing. We all know, from acute personal experience, that risk can bring both reward and devastation. And the difference between the two outcomes can often seem arbitrary. Healthy, well-adjusted people seem to have forged a tenuous balance between risk and prudence. But even though we are on a perpetual quest for that balance, there is no formula for it, and the stakes are high. So we weigh the consequences of our risk, and the older we get, the more our balance tips toward the safety of disengagement. We've seen too much. We know too much. And as a result, we "manage our risk" so well that we choke off the fuel our soul needs to stay alive—because taking risks is integral to our spiritual vitality.

> In the same way that God has created us to be dependent on oxygen for our physical survival, He has created us to be dependent on risk for our soul's survival.

Through all great literature and storytelling, there runs the universal thread of a main character who's uniquely ill-prepared for heroic deeds but who must meet the challenge nevertheless. Pick a favorite book or film—anything from *Don Quixote* to *The Hobbit* or *To Kill a Mockingbird* to *The Hunger Games*—and you'll run right into the "unlikely hero" archetype. Why? Because something inside us resonates with this core storyline. We have an addiction to the David-and-Goliath theme that shows up consistently in the stories we love—a theme so compelling that we can't resist its "high."

Could it be that God himself has embedded *ordinary-but-heroic* in our soul's DNA as a siren call, beckoning us onward as we run our race? And could it therefore be that Jesus' words, "Whoever loses his life for My sake will find it," are among the sweetest words we'll ever hear? His words call the hero in us out from the shadows of the ordinary, urging us—to paraphrase missionary/martyr Jim Elliot—to give what we cannot keep in order to gain what we cannot lose.[3] After all, love would not be love that lowered its hopes to a settled life of "quiet desperation."

So what is the meaning of my life and your life?

However we may have answered this question in the past, a close examination of our responses will reveal an undeniable truth: to varying degrees, they all ring hollow. Most of the ways we evaluate our intrinsic value leave us with a bitter aftertaste. Professional success? Financial success? Being a good person? The pursuit of happiness? The American Dream? None of these satisfy. Even the relative few of us who say we "have it all" feel unfulfilled by what we've got and what we've achieved. A lot is never enough, and "more" never delivers on its hype.

How do we handle that? Typically, lacking a bedrock of significance for our lives, we act as if whatever ground we happen to occupy will suffice: "I always dreamed of playing professionally, but watching it on TV is as close as I'm going to get." "I'd always hoped to make it as a screenwriter, but a person can only handle so much rejection—and anyway, my degree, you know, is in business administration. It pays the bills and [conspiratorial wink] the mortgage on our condo in Hawaii."

Or we distract ourselves from the question of meaning altogether. Situated in the rich excesses of postmodern living, most of us have all the resources we need to pursue our distractions for a lifetime, and many of us do.

Yet we have moments.

Moments when we wonder about the unmet hunger inside us.

Times when we feel an uncomfortable stirring, even a desperation, to discover whether there is something more congruent with our soul's longings than the false rewards of "the good life."

And when we look to Jesus, slowing down to study the provocative ways He engaged the needy, wounded, and desperate people who surrounded Him, we find the certain answer we crave.

God Has Chosen to Need Us

This truth is core to our identity and our purpose in life. And God refuses to back down on it. He wants our "skin in the game"; otherwise, it's game-over for our soul.

Of course, the God who is omnipotent, omniscient, and omnipresent *could* choose to work alone. But instead, He elects (at great cost to Himself) to move through a body of people. He has done so from the dawn of time, and He is doing so now—through men and women like you and me who are far less prepared for kingdom-of-God adventures than Don Quixote or Bilbo or Atticus or Katniss were for their own exploits. *It is no stretch to say that God simply will not operate unilaterally.* Instead, He moves through and with willing partners. He insists that we offer the treasure of our *risk* as the admission price to the mother of all adventures: the beautiful advance of His kingdom and the epic redemption of His people.

With determination, God invites us to make His missional purposes our own. We see this repeatedly in Jesus' encounters with ordinary men and women:

- In the John 9 story of the man blind from birth, Jesus smears a mixture of dirt and spit on the man's eyes, then tells him to go to the pool of Siloam to wash away a lifetime of darkness. What gets lost in this odd and remarkable story of healing is this: Jesus asks a blind man with spit-mud on his face to find his own way through town to a pool, where he can complete the process of healing. Why? Would *you* force the man through such an unnecessary gauntlet of shame and uncertainty? Of course not. But Jesus wanted the man's skin in the game.

- In the John 5 story of the crippled man who has languished by the pool of Bethesda for thirty-eight years, Jesus asks a question so obvious that it is either ridiculous or offensive or both: "Do you want to be healed?"

   Of course he does. That's why he's there. Everyone in town knows why scores of sick people wait by the poolside. Periodically, an angel of God stirs the water. The man hopes to be the first one in, thus finding healing for his lameness. Yet Jesus still insists on asking, "What do you want?"

   The non-negotiable here looms large: the man must give evidence that he has skin in the game before Jesus will offer him what he says he wants most. And the man rises to the challenge: "Yes! I want to be healed."

- In Matthew 15, the Canaanite woman grovels, pleading with Jesus to heal her daughter of demon possession. But the Master first ignores her, and then when he does turn his attention to her, it is with apparent scorn: "It is not good to take the children's bread and throw it to the dogs " (v. 26).

   Where's the love in a response like that? For a moment, the air is thick with awkward silence. But Jesus' true motive behind His question is revealed in the woman's reply and His own response to it.

   "Even the dogs eat the crumbs that fall from their master's table," she answers.

"Woman, you have great faith!" He says. "Your request is granted."

Jesus' purposeful offense demands that the woman put her skin in the game—and when she does, He is delighted, and His heart toward her becomes clear (vv. 27–28 NIV).

We have only scratched the surface of these uncomfortable and curious encounters. In every instance, Jesus asks those who would follow Him to be co-participants in His work. He will kick in the $105,000 seed, contingent only on our feeble but mandatory hundred dollars. Ours is the "widow's mite"—but it is also the coin that He's decided will ultimately tip the scales.

This truth answers so many of our questions about God's movement in our lives. God will not do alone what He chooses to do with us. Yet we are often unwilling to accept, or are simply unaware, that our *risky and personal investment* is a prerequisite.

> We do not give ourselves over to Jesus, body and soul, without a fight. That is why He coaxes us out of our bunker mentality with eight forceful questions. These questions drag us out of our unconscious passivity and, if we choose, entice us to step out of our security zones into the epic, Jesus-centered adventure we were made for.

Behind the mysterious biblical accounts of Jesus' encounters with the "quietly desperate," you'll find a question in each of the following eight chapters. But they're not just the stuff of which great Bible stories are made. We, too, are confronted with them repeatedly in our everyday lives. And how we answer them will determine whether we experience the life God intends for us or the life we are tempted to merely endure. Risk is merely our turning of the knob on a wardrobe door that opens into Narnia.

FOR DISCUSSION OR PERSONAL REFLECTION

- On a 1-to-10 continuum between "Safety" and "Risk," where would you put yourself, based on the way you live your life? What are the primary reasons why you are there?
- If you were audited by an impartial angel who had access to every nook and cranny of your life, in what areas would that angel determine you have skin in the game, and in what areas would he determine you've been averse to taking "good risks"? Why is there divergence in these areas?
- Which "unlikely hero" from a film, book, play, or song resonates with you most strongly, and why?
- In the table of contents, which one of the eight questions that make up the chapter titles draws your interest the most, and why? Which one makes you feel particularly fearful, and why?

CHAPTER 1

WILL YOU FACE YOUR SHAME?

*The Story of the Notorious Woman
and the Accidental Well*

*"It is the false shame of fools to try to conceal wounds that
have not healed."*

—Horace

When I was fifteen years old, my family made its triennial trek from Denver across the Kansas Serengeti to visit my mother's relatives in Missouri. I hadn't seen my cousins in a few years, so I was a little startled to see Debbie, who is six years older than I, walking with a noticeable limp. Actually, it was more dramatic than a limp. When she walked, she literally dragged her left leg behind her, swinging it forward as if it had gone to sleep.

I vaguely remembered someone telling me that she had some sort of chronic disorder (multiple sclerosis, I found out later), but back then, the only thing that mattered in my teenage-guy world was a particular kind of currency called humor. My cultural pantheon started and ended with Monty Python. So early on in our visit, walking behind Debbie down a sidewalk toward the car, I decided to spend a little of my humor currency: I mocked Debbie's exaggerated gait by dragging my leg, just like she did. I laughed at myself and quickly looked around to make sure the others had noticed my comic brilliance. They had—but they weren't laughing. And, suddenly, the reality of what I'd done sank in.

The shame was almost instantaneous. My face burning, I begged God to let me go back in time so I could erase those five seconds of cruelty. Instead, I wallowed in my sin for the rest of my family's visit. I feel the faint burn of shame even now when I describe my inexplicable behavior.

It all happened almost four decades ago, but the details are etched forever in my memory. That's because shame leaves an indelible imprint on us. Like Shakespeare's Lady Macbeth, we cry, "Out, damned spot!" as we try—and fail—to rub away the stain from our soiled hands.

Shame is an unforgiving master. It taunts our God-given identity, bullying us into a life of hiding and caution. Shame reorients our reality by distorting how we see ourselves and the people who relate to us.

For one long-ago woman of Samaria, shame was what caused her to venture out in the middle of the day, when the sun beat its hottest on the cracked earth, to draw water from the community water source outside the city walls of Sychar.

Picture her heading toward Jacob's Well. Why does she choose this time? Because she's a notorious woman, a target for the kind of murderous whispers that kill the soul, and now is the time when she's least likely to encounter other townspeople.

But today, someone else does show up. Left alone by his disciples, who are in town scouting for supplies, Jesus is sitting at the well when the woman arrives to draw water. He's tired, hot, and thirsty, and he asks her to give Him a drink. But his request quickly surfaces a cautious response that is rooted in the shame of her ethnicity and her gender and her reputation. "How is it that You, being a Jew, ask me for a drink since I am a Samaritan woman?" she asks (John 4:9).

In response, Jesus tells her that she has, essentially, hit the jackpot: standing before her is the Source of "living water," the kind she can drink and then never thirst again. Her hope kindled, the woman begs Jesus for some of that water. For her, it represents freedom from having to travel to the well, where every day she is reminded that she is a serial-rejected woman and an outcast living under the shadow of her shame. So instead of skirting her shame, Jesus draws it out like a poison: "'Go, call your husband and come here.' The woman answered and said, 'I have no husband.' Jesus said to her, 'You have correctly said, "I have no husband"; for you have had five husbands, and the one whom you now have is not your husband; this you have said truly'" (John 4:16–18).

Now the woman must decide what she will do: face her shame or shrink from it. Will she drink what Jesus is offering her or do what most of us would do and make an excuse to cover her retreat? It's the choice all of us who would enter into the life Jesus invites us into must make. Will we stop hiding *in* our shame and *from* our shame and instead drag it into the light, where it can no longer leverage us? Because the adventure Jesus beckons us into is lived out in the light. There is no darkness in Him, and everything that lives in the shadows will be called out of hiding. "For nothing is hidden that will not become evident, nor *anything* secret that will not be known and come to light" (Luke 8:17). On the journey that will lead us, ultimately, to freely offer our skin in the game, the first question Jesus asks us is both simple and terrible: "Will you face your shame?"

> Put another way, Jesus is asking, "Will you come out and play?"

When we are young, responding to the invitation to "come out and play" is as natural as breathing. But over time, our play response is hampered and even destroyed by the progressive advance of shame through our soul's fortifications—the mortar fire of everyday life blows holes in our walls, making it seem unsafe to play. Of course, original sin is just another way of saying that we are all born into a kind of fundamental shame, and life's embarrassments and indignities and failures quickly accelerate its impact on us. Our fundamental shame is like a roadside bomb—it has latent explosive capability that is released when something in the external environment triggers it, causing indiscriminate collateral damage. In other words, shame blows our legs out from under us, making us all "disabled" in the truest sense.

Shame's impact grows over time for a simple reason: just living in a fallen world exposes us to an environment fraught with things that can trigger shame. This is why so many of us suffer from social anxiety disorder, whose defining characteristic is the "fear of negative evaluation by others." Shame is a worldwide epidemic. In the Asian world, for example, shame and "saving face" are primary psycho-social forces, shaping the soul of both the individual and the culture. The Japanese have a word, *hazukashii*,[1] for the cultural expectation that one must at all costs avoid bringing shame to the family name. In Chinese culture, there are 113 unique shame terms embedded in the language.[2]

Harvard researchers have boiled it down to this: "Shame functions as a social control mechanism that makes use of the emotion's aversive properties." In other words, shame exerts a powerful leverage on us.

The Psychology of Shame: A Thumbnail Sketch

Dr. Allan Schore serves on the clinical faculty of the Department of Psychiatry and Behavioral Sciences at UCLA. His research into the factors that fuel *attachment theory* sheds light on the foundations of our shame. Attachment theory is a psychological construct that explores why an infant *must* develop a close relationship with at least one primary caregiver in order for social and emotional development to advance normally.

Researchers have discovered that, contrary to conventional wisdom, our genetics are *not* set in concrete at birth. There is far more genetic material in an infant's brain at ten months, say, than at birth. Schore says, "One of the great fallacies that many scientists have is that everything that is before birth is genetic and that everything that is after birth is learned. This is not the case."[3] The part of the brain that is core (or "primitive") is the brain stem, and it's the *only* part of the brain that is fully developed at birth. The rest continues to form at a rapid pace over the first two years of life as the neurons develop a protective sheath and establish connections with each other. This two-year construction project is highly influenced by environmental factors—"triggers" that surround us as we grow into toddlers. And, by far, our primary caregivers control the lion's share of them.

Clinical psychologist and author Joseph Burgo says, "When things go wrong between parent and child in the first two years of life, you [the child] are permanently damaged by it in ways that cannot be erased. The awareness that you are damaged, the felt knowledge that you didn't get what you needed and that as a result, your emotional development has been warped and stunted in profound ways—this is what I refer to as *basic shame*."[4]

The reality is that basic shame—or what I've called "fundamental shame"—is inescapable for everyone born into a world profoundly altered by sin. On a spiritual level, our "birth canal" was filled with toxic water. Not a person on earth has escaped the sin bath, and once we come sputtering out of it, much lies in wait for us to trigger our shame: A mother, damaged herself, feels exasperated by her infant daughter rather than delighted. An uncle, sick with a shattered soul, touches a helpless little boy in sexually abusive ways. A father, stressed by his responsibilities and hollowed out by hidden sins, unfavorably compares his little girl to her "little blonde pixie" best friend. These indiscriminate and often unintended incidents create "subluxations" in our core identity which alter the way we see ourselves, others, and God.

Subluxations and the Chiropractic of Shame

In the world of chiropractic, a subluxation is a misalignment in the spine that affects one's neural performance. When you have a subluxation, your nervous system's normal functioning is compromised, much like a clogged fuel jet in a carburetor leads to a sputtering engine. And a "sputtering" spinal column can lead to all sorts of problems we normally associate with medical conditions that require prescription drugs or surgery.

Chiropractors rouse the suspicions of the medical community because they speak a kind of heresy: *Instead of medicating the problem, most conditions can be treated by fixing the subluxation that caused it.*

In Romans 1:19-20, the apostle Paul says, in essence, that everything in the created world is a parable about who God is and how He operates. These parables are embedded by God in His creation, waiting to be discovered. So maybe subluxations of the spine can teach us something about another kind of subluxation—the misalignments in our soul caused by shame; the degenerative subluxations that keep us from functioning as God intended and living freely out of our truest identity.

Is it possible for us to experience a realignment of our soul—a kind of spiritual chiropractic adjustment that allows us to overcome the damage shame has caused?

Experts such as Dr. Burgo say such damage cannot be erased. Burgo explains, "Cognitive-behavior therapy might teach you some useful techniques for coping with your damage, but it won't make you into a different person. No matter what you do, you'll never be just like the person who went through the emotional experiences she needed during that critical period. . . . Toxic shame so poisons one's sense of self that the usual remedy is flight into various types of narcissistic behavior."[5]

Apparently, we cannot gain back the shameless, clean slate we had in the womb—the pristine identity that was "fearfully and wonderfully made" in the image of God. We cannot climb back into our mother's womb and go through the birthing process again, can we?

That is exactly the objection a Pharisee named Nicodemus raised when Jesus told him, matter-of-factly, "Truly, truly, I say to you, unless one is born again he cannot see the kingdom of God" (John 3:3).

It helps to slow down and pay better attention to what Jesus is saying here. We cannot "see" the kingdom of God unless we are born again—and that is because our basic shame, compounded by the thousands of trigger experiences of shame we encounter in our life, clouds our soul's lens and taints everything we see. A rebirth is our only hope—but not simply a rebirth into the same world of sin and shame we've already experienced. We need a rebirth into a new world—a world called the kingdom of God. It sounds ridiculous, but this is what Jesus offers the woman he meets at the well outside of Sychar.

Five Minutes with Jesus by a Well Outside of Sychar

The Samaritan woman's story of hope is our story of hope. It is possible to move past the dead end of our shame and into the wide thoroughfare of our true identity and our strategic purpose in the kingdom of God. It is possible not merely to cope with our damage but to become a regenerated person. It is possible for us to *see* the kingdom of God, and therefore, it is also possible for us to put our skin in its game.

Let's camp for a moment in the experience of the notorious woman of Sychar in John 4:3–42 and find from her journey with

Jesus the trail markers for our own journey. We'll carefully consider each move in their verbal chess match.

1. *"Give Me a drink."*

Jesus is the shrewdest man who ever walked the earth, and so he begins His benevolent attack on the woman's shame with an invitation to serve Him. He knows, as we generally do not, that He can find the leverage He needs to pry open our soul and expose the dark beliefs we hide about ourselves by simply asking us to help Him.

Right away, we must wrestle with feelings of unworthiness that lead to doubt and caution. When Dr. Brené Brown, a research professor at the University of Houston's graduate college of social work, first gave a twenty-minute presentation on the necessity of vulnerability for living a "whole-hearted life" at a 2011 TED conference, she woke up the next morning gripped with shame and anxiety. For the five hundred people in attendance and, later, the four million who watched her presentation on YouTube (making it the most-watched TED talk of all time), Dr. Brown's bare-faced revelations about her own struggles with vulnerability were a life-giving revelation. But for her, like the woman standing by the well outside Sychar, the act of giving what she had to give unleashed a raging torrent of shame.

"Shame drives two big tapes," says Brown: "'Never good enough' and, if you can talk yourself out of that one, 'Who do you think you are?'"[6] When we are asked to give and we do, we are certain to wrestle with the dragon called shame that has been summoned from our dungeon. Jesus knows what He's doing when He asks us to serve Him.

2. *"How is it that You, being a Jew, ask me for a drink since I am a Samaritan woman?"*

Put another way, the woman is asking Jesus: "Do you know who I am, really? I am obviously the sort of person you should not be talking to—Jews like you treat people like me like scurvy dogs, and my gender alone should make me off-limits to you." The incredulity we have about our own worth or status exposes the shame that is driving our beliefs—the poison we've ingested is driven to the surface.

3. *"If you knew the gift of God, and who it is who says to you, 'Give Me a drink,' you would have asked Him, and He would have given you living water."*

When we have started to admit what we really believe about ourselves, Jesus turns the tables. In effect, He tells us, "I already know who you are to the depths of your soul, but you know next to nothing about Me. If you had an inkling of My goodness and the rich treasures I long to give You, you'd be desperate for Me. But you won't ask, because your shame won't let you receive anything from Me." Jesus offers us a taste of what our soul most craves, dangling it in front of us, enticing us to come out of the shadows and into the light.

4. *"Sir, You have nothing to draw with and the well is deep; where then do You get that living water? You are not greater than our father Jacob, are You, who gave us the well, and drank of it himself and his sons and his cattle?"*

It's a certainty that we will, at least initially, push back against the invitation Jesus offers us by questioning His ability to give us what we really need. In essence, we can't help but test His promises to us, because shame has taught us that most people in our life don't keep most of their promises most of the time—at least, the promises that really matter to us. Is Jesus really able to deliver what He's offering? If my other caregivers failed to wholly love me, why should I trust a God who has not proven Himself to me? And if other "experts" have taken their best shot at helping me and failed, why should I expect a different result from a Jesus who talks big but may not have the capacity to deliver?

5. *"Everyone who drinks of this water will thirst again; but whoever drinks of the water that I will give him shall never thirst; but the water that I will give him will become in him a well of water springing up to eternal life."*

Here Jesus separates Himself from all our other caregivers. He tells us, bluntly, that the many solutions we've pursued to heal our shame are at best temporary fixes. The people we've trusted before have all failed us in one way or another. The "good life" turns out to be a hollow pursuit with quickly diminishing returns. (This helps explain why the United States has the highest suicide rate in the world, even though we also have the highest standard of living in world history.)

But Jesus offers a permanent fix—an ongoing and refreshing source of identity that will finally quench our thirst. He makes a bold statement of ability and outcome. Is it too good to be true? This is the tipping point He brings us to. We stand on the divide between the path of retreat and the path of advance. Will we capitulate to our shame, or face it and extend our hand to grasp the already-extended hand of Jesus?

6. *"Sir, give me this water, so I will not be thirsty nor come all the way here to draw."*

The woman takes the biggest risk of her life—she allows her desperate thirst to overrule her desperate shame. She asks for what Jesus is offering. This is more vulnerable and risky than a quick reading of this encounter assumes. This is a woman convinced of her unworthiness, so allowing herself to hope is perhaps the bravest thing she's ever done. In fact, asking for what we've always believed is impossible may be the most vulnerable thing any of us will ever do and therefore the most courageous thing we'll ever do.

"I've come to the belief," says Brené Brown, "that vulnerability is our most accurate measurement of courage."[7] And so the woman by the well is taking the road less travelled by facing down her shame and boldly asking for what she most wants. But she hedges a little, too; she wants her thirst to be quenched, and she also wants to hunker down at home and avoid the embarrassment and pain of the crowd's whispered judgments.

7. *"Go, call your husband and come here."*
Jesus, it turns out, refuses to offer partial solutions to our problem of shame. When we barter with Him for safer alternatives to His redemptive mission in our lives, He will not negotiate. Instead, He targets the thing we've kept well-hidden, the thing we swore we'd keep buried forever. He wants us to face it.

8. *"I have no husband."*
The woman fudges the truth about her situation with a half-truth that hides her brutal reality. Like her, we will do anything to avoid fully facing our shame—and we are well-skilled at evading others' pursuit of it. So we equivocate and stall and dull the edges of the knife's blade: "Can I take a pill instead of surgery?" And Jesus, instead, produces a scalpel.

Jim Stockdale was an officer and prisoner of war in the infamous "Hanoi Hilton" during the Vietnam War. He was imprisoned for eight years, from 1965 to 1973, and was relentlessly and ruthlessly tortured. But he survived the experience, and the way that he survived has now been studied and taught around the world. It's called the Stockdale Paradox.[8] The key to survival, as author Jim Collins framed Stockdale's experience, is this: "You must never confuse faith that you will prevail in the end—which you can never afford to lose—with the discipline to confront the most brutal facts of your current reality, whatever they might be."

Jesus operates, all of the time, in the tension described by the Stockdale Paradox. He will move us to face the "most brutal facts of our current reality, whatever they might be." But He reassures us with absolute certainty that we will "prevail in the end."

9. "You have correctly said, 'I have no husband'; for you have had five husbands, and the one whom you now have is not your husband; this you have said truly."

Jesus not only points out her shame, He rubs her nose in it. That's because, for her and for us, shame must become an acknowledged reality before He can confront it. We can't give Him permission to heal us if we don't admit the truth about our "disease." And the truth is, we don't merely have a shame-cold—we have shame-cancer.

One way we know Jesus is "not of this world" is this: when we would back away from a wound that is so tender it hurts us to look at it, He pushes into that wound instead. He's intent on healing us, not serving up hollow platitudes that ignore the obvious, festering side effects of our sickness. Once the truth of our shame is in the open, we can invite the sort of treatment that matches the disease.

That is why Jesus relentlessly dismantles our hiding strategies—because, as Dr. Brown says, "[Shame] needs three things to grow exponentially: secrecy, silence, and judgment."[9] All three forces are at play in the Samaritan woman's life. And exposure to the blinding light of truth is the only force strong enough to counter them.

But Jesus is not the sort of physician who says, "I know what's wrong with you, and I'm going to treat you whether or not you want Me to." He wants our invitation.

10. "Sir, I perceive that You are a prophet. . . . I know that Messiah is coming (He who is called Christ); when that One comes, He will declare all things to us."

Jesus has just hauled her shame into unwavering light, and it's humiliating to have something so ugly exposed. What do we do when our hidden ugly becomes our outer ugly?

We could make an excuse and slink away. Or we could blow up and demand an apology. Or we could turn the tables and try to defame our defamer. Or . . .

We could give in to the truth, accept the reality of our shame, and name our Healer.

When we decide to let Jesus do something about our shame, we will always name Him Lord and Messiah. It's a statement not only about His identity but also about our posture toward Him. It's the bended knee of faith—faith in His ability to do what He promises because of who He is. And faith is not something we work up; it's a truth we desperately embrace. So, when we name Him "Messiah," we are offering Him access to our soul's most vulnerable places as He hovers over them, holding His scalpel.

11. "I who speak to you am He."

Jesus asserts His true identity—and more. He assures us that he has the power, authority, and skill to get the job done. He not only offers us living water, but He also delivers on that promise. What psychology, self-discipline, and determination can't do on their own, He can do. And the proof of it, here by the well outside Sychar, is that a woman who has long lived in a prison of shame—the same woman who has been written off and marginalized in the public square—heads back inside the city walls to tell even her detractors that they too can find hope for healing their shame if they'll drink the living water of the man by the well. She is a new creation because she has taken a big gulp of that living water. And so the last person you'd expect to tell anyone about the Messiah becomes the first Christian evangelist in history. She is "born again"—and that is a miracle.

The Reiteration of Paradise

Despite his assertion that basic shame is irreversible, Dr. Burgo does claim that a long-term relationship with a psychotherapist (who models healthier responses than the narcissism most of us default to) can blunt shame's influence enough to make it tolerable. But this is only a faint echo of the bellowing voice of Jesus telling us we must be born again and offering us living water—which is, in the end, really Himself. His promise is "paradise"—it's the gift he offered Dismas, the name given to the thief on the cross who defended Jesus before a mocking crowd and received Jesus' promise, "Today you will be with me in paradise" (Luke 23:43 NIV).

The words "with me in paradise" are, functionally, a reiteration. I mean, "with me" and "paradise" are really the same thing when the Me is Jesus. To be with Him—not in a geographical sense but in a spiritual and more romantic sense—is to be in paradise.

Paradise is actually a transliteration of the Greek word *paradeisos*, which is rooted in the Old Persian word *pairidaeza*, meaning "enclosure." More literally, it refers to the garden of God in the creation story (Gen. 2:8-10, 15). What if the garden of Eden, the place where Adam and Eve walked with God "in the cool of the evening," is not only hovered over by the Spirit of Jesus but is a representation of Jesus Himself? And what if the intoxicating scent of Jesus that we sniff when He confronts us with our shame lures us out of our smelly prison into the paradise of His presence? There is a pathway into God's garden, where we can wholeheartedly offer up our skin in the game, but we must leave our shame at the gate. He will help us do it, if we let Him.

FOR DISCUSSION OR PERSONAL REFLECTION

- Close your eyes and ask God to take you back to what might be called a "moment of shame" in your life. How did that experience impact you in the short and long terms?
- How did your parents help you feel either less or more fundamental shame in your life? Condense your answer into a single sentence.
- What are some ways in which you relate to the woman at the well? What are some ways you find it hard to relate to her?
- Is it generally easy or hard for you to trust God? What's the main reason why?

- How do you find Dr. Brown's statement that "vulnerability is our most accurate measurement of courage" true in your own life?
- Reflecting on your life, what are some ways Jesus has dragged your shame into the light? What happened when He did?
- How have you been drawn more deeply into relationship with Jesus as you have struggled with the side effects of shame in your life?

CHAPTER 2

WILL YOU RECEIVE GRACE?

The Story of the Offended Servant and the Degraded King

> *"We can only do God's will when we realize our own utter helplessness, ignorance, and inability to cope with life."*
>
> —William Barclay

"Never shall You wash my feet!"

It is the Last Supper, and this is the headstrong and self-conscious vow of a man who's well aware of his secret sins, his checkered past, and his low upbringing. He is Peter, and in John 13:3–10, he will not accept an honor that he does not deserve. He knows his place.

Peter's equation is most often ours as well: admit it or not, we want no honor we have not earned and no responsibilities that aren't equal to our station in life. Had Peter been asked to wash Jesus' feet, Peter would have done so without thinking. After all, the lesser is *supposed* to serve the greater. But the reverse of this act of subservience is unthinkable to him. And so, Jesus responds to Peter's stubbornness: "If I do not wash you, you have no part with Me." In essence, Jesus is telling Peter that he won't be allowed to partner with Him in His kingdom-of-God adventures if Peter refuses to receive the grace he's been offered.

> Our own refusal to receive God's grace is, like Peter's, a determination to deserve whatever we gain—and this automatically excludes us from investing our skin in the game.

In our relationship with Jesus, there is no aspect that is not dependent upon grace. Receiving God's grace is our ticket into the missional activities of the kingdom of God. And once Peter understands this truth, he makes a quick about-face. He's desperate to join Jesus in whatever He's doing, and he's determined to prove his willingness to go all-in with Him: "Lord, then wash not only my feet, but also my hands and my head."

Our highest form of arrogance is also the most deeply camouflaged, and Jesus must smoke it out of the shadows by offering us His grace as the entryway into His presence. He will ask us to relax and release our white-knuckled grip on our own relative "goodness" so that we can channel His goodness instead. And He will do much to expose our self-righteousness and entice us to take a risk on His righteousness instead.

This truth is embedded in the most famous of Jesus' parables: the Prodigal Son (Luke 15:11–32). Really, though, the parable is about two sons, not one.

In the story, the younger son wants nothing to do with his father; in fact, he'd be just fine if his father dropped dead. But because he's unwilling to wait for that happy day, he asks for his inheritance ahead of time so he can permanently leave his father's house behind him and make his own way in life. The younger son represents the sort of shameless arrogance that makes no excuses for its hubris. He is rough and hard and angry and wounded and stubborn and given over to sin. He wants nothing to do with his father, treating him like a vending machine that has not given the correct change.

The older son is nothing like his reprobate sibling. He's sticking it out at home, toiling away in the relative boredom of his everyday responsibilities. In contrast to his scandalous brother, he is obedient and hard-working and upstanding and loyal. He is also—though he doesn't realize it—smug in his self-righteousness. He tells himself, "I'm no blackguard like my younger brother."

It is only when the father is caught up in celebrating the younger son's repentance and redemption that the older son's lost-ness is revealed. He's furious that his good-for-nothing brother is so quickly welcomed back into his father's graces and, even more, that his father intends to lavish the younger son with an extravagant party.

The story ends with the younger son redeemed but the older son not redeemed. And I think we have it backward: the hardhearted son in this story is really the older one. In the end, he is the one who refuses to be in relationship with his father because He is profoundly offended by grace.

The Ghost and the Bleeding Charity

In C. S. Lewis's masterwork, *The Great Divorce*, the Oxford don brilliantly translates the dynamics of camouflaged arrogance into a gripping sub-narrative.

In the book, a bus from heaven shows up in hell, offering the inhabitants a chance to take a field trip back to heaven, where they can perhaps transfer their residence. The bus quickly fills up with ghosts who are all convinced, in one way or another, that they don't belong in hell.

After this motley lot of characters disembarks from the bus, they experience individual encounters with various inhabitants of

heaven—"bright spirits," Lewis calls them—who extend God's offer
of grace at the risk that it will very likely be refused.

In one such encounter, the bright spirit turns out to be a man
who once worked for the ghost when the two were both alive. The
ghost is offended that the bright spirit, formerly a convicted murderer, now is a citizen of heaven thanks to the grace of Christ, while
the ghost has been sentenced to hell—unfairly, he insists.

> "Look at me, now," said the Ghost, slapping its chest (but
> the slap made no noise). "I gone straight all my life. I don't
> say I was a religious man and I don't say I had no faults, far
> from it. But I done my best all my life, see? I done my best by
> everyone, that's the sort of chap I was. I never asked for any-
> thing that wasn't mine by rights. If I wanted a drink I paid
> for it and if I took my wages I done my job, see? That's the
> sort I was and I don't care who knows it."
>
> "It would be much better not to go on about that now."
>
> "Who's going on? I'm not arguing. I'm just telling you the
> sort of chap I was, see? I'm asking for nothing but my rights.
> You may think you can put me down because you're dressed
> up like that (which you weren't when you worked under me)
> and I'm only a poor man. But I got to have my rights same
> as you, see?"
>
> "Oh no. It's not so bad as that. I haven't got my rights, or
> I should not be here. You will not get yours either. You'll get
> something far better. Never fear."
>
> "That's just what I say. I haven't got my rights. I always
> done my best and I never done nothing wrong. And what
> I don't see is why I should be put below a bloody murderer
> like you."
>
> "Who knows whether you will be? Only be happy and
> come with me."
>
> "What do you keep on arguing for? I'm only telling you

the sort of chap I am. I only want my rights. I'm not asking for anybody's bleeding charity."

"Then do. At once. Ask for the Bleeding Charity. Everything is here for the asking and nothing can be bought."[1]

In the kingdom of God, we can ask for anything, but we can buy nothing—a humbling prospect, for we are never comfortable unless we are in control. We hate it when our currency can't get us the thing we seek, because we want to gain what we seek by right of purchase. But grace can't be bought, no matter what currency we offer for it. That's why it is a delicacy only the desperate hunger for, and the desperate have long since decoupled themselves from their "rights," just as a hiker will leave his backpack behind when he is chased by a bear.

When you think about the interactions Jesus had, the stories He told, and the life He lived, you'll see that human desperation is the theme that runs through all of them. It's really a central aspect of Jesus' relationships. It's a primary theme in the parable of the prodigal son. For that matter, it's a hallmark of nearly every good novel, film, or TV show, because we're fascinated by how people in the midst of desperate circumstances respond to them.

We almost always know the apparent causes of why we ourselves feel desperate: a lost job, financial trouble, rejection, a child struggling with an addiction. But we may not discern the root of our desperation at a deeper level. We find its source, however, when we track human history all the way back to Adam and Eve.

Adam and Eve gave in to the temptation of sin because they wanted to be equal to God.

Now the serpent was more crafty than any of the wild animals the LORD God had made. He said to the woman, "Did God really say, 'You must not eat from any tree in the garden'?"

The woman said to the serpent, "We may eat fruit from

the trees in the garden, but God did say, 'You must not eat fruit from the tree that is in the middle of the garden, and you must not touch it, or you will die.'"

"You will not certainly die," the serpent said to the woman. "For God knows that when you eat from it your eyes will be opened, and you will be like God, knowing good and evil." (Gen. 3:1–5 NIV)

Satan promises Eve that she can become like God, self-sufficient and in charge of her own destiny. It's a deal she can't refuse. Adam quickly follows her lead. Together, they put their faith in the false hope that they can be gods.

But in the kingdom of God, if you believe you're a god, you separate yourself from relationship with the one true God. We're literally sick with the myth of our own self-sufficiency. Desperate dependence on God serves as a medicine that can help make us well. It reminds us that we're not God; we never have been, we're not right now, and we never will be. It tells us we're not in control.

The Fount of Temptation

In the thick of the new millennium's worldwide economic downturn, when more American families had lost their homes and jobs than any generation since the Great Depression, the specter of financial disaster washed over millions of people like an acid-bath, stripping them to their core. One day during the nadir of the meltdown, listening to the public radio show *Marketplace* as I drove home from work, I heard host Kai Ryssdal offer a nugget of conventional wisdom as a teaser to an upcoming story about financially ruined Californians who were returning to church in droves.

He said, "When all else fails, there's faith."

Expanded, Ryssdal's casual maxim translates like this: *Once you've responsibly exhausted all of your own resources, you may feel humiliated enough to try anything, no matter how ridiculous it may seem under normal circumstances.* We do not easily give over control of our life to the crapshoot of faith. We have been slaves to the tyranny of our own control for so long that we can't imagine what freedom might feel like.

In an episode of the spooky old show *The X-Files*, the sinister "Cigarette Smoking Man" channeled the voice of Satan when he said, "We give them happiness and they give us authority, the authority to take away their freedom under the guise of democracy. Men can never be free. They're weak, corrupt, worthless, and restless. The people believe in authority. They've grown tired of waiting for miracle and mystery. Science is their religion. No greater explanation exists for them. They must never believe any differently if the project is to go forward."[2]

The "project" is an apt metaphor for our own little man-made hell—a place where the grace of spiritual freedom has been overrun by pragmatic survivalism and capitulation to control. Only desperate circumstances offer a way out. Like Dismas hanging on the cross, we turn to Jesus only when we ourselves are being crucified.

When my kids were little, I would hold them in the crook of my arm as I walked from the shallow end of our neighborhood swimming pool into the deep end. As the water crept up around us, they would cling to me more tightly. And this always gave me a profound sense of intimacy with my daughters. The deepening water forced the false hubris of independence out of them, replacing it with the stark reality of their desperate dependence. The deeper the water, the more my daughters squeezed their little bodies into the refuge of my strength.

That's how it is with us and God. When we walk with Him into the deep end of our lives, we find sanctuary in His strength as our own sense of independence fades. Rescue drives us closer to Jesus, and closeness is what God is after. God wants us to live with desperate dependence upon Him, because He longs to draw us near.

But He will first have to expose, then undermine, then starve our hunger for control. This is what paves the way for us to finally offer our skin in the game. He is inviting us into a desperately dependent relationship that is abandoned to Him and marked by both an easy intimacy and a fierce sense of our kingdom-of-God purpose.

The dependence we hate is the dependence we desperately need; it is the antidote to a life dominated by the insidious demands of being in control. What would happen if we lost ourselves by relinquishing the control we so staunchly defend? Jesus says that, paradoxically, we will actually find ourselves: "For whoever wishes to [control] his life will lose it; but whoever [gives over control of] his life for My sake will find it" (Matt. 16:25).

We are not truly masters of our domain, no matter how hard we try to convince ourselves otherwise. When Peter invites rather than resists Jesus' radical offer of grace, his act of dependence frees him from the prison of his own control and plunges him more deeply into the intimacy with Jesus that he wants above all other things. There is a way to escape the tyranny of our camouflaged self-righteousness, and Jesus not only shows us the path, but He *is* the path.

Traveling Outside of Karma

The iconic rock band U2, and its primary songwriter, Bono, have a knack for exegeting biblical truths and then burying them, like parables, in their songs. "Grace" is one of those songs. In it, Bono personifies grace as both a world-changing thought and as the name of a woman. Bono describes her as a woman who "travels outside of karma."

Karma is an Eastern religious concept embraced by both Hinduism and Buddhism. It means, essentially, that we get what we deserve. It's the same message we've told our kids at Christmas: "If you're good, you'll get. If you're not, you won't."

Grace, on the other hand, runs counter to what we deserve. And though we generally embrace grace as a concept and don't openly embrace Eastern religious thought in our lives, Western Christians most certainly embrace the idea of karma. The majority of us in the Western world still believe that the way we get to heaven is to be good people—for example, a Barna Research Group study found that 54 percent of Americans believe that if people are generally good, or do enough good things for others during their life, they'll earn a place in heaven.[3] We get what we deserve. Many more of us who know "the right answer"—that faith in Christ, and therefore redemption in Christ, is the only path to heaven—nevertheless functionally live as if our invitation into heaven depends on our own goodness.

I was talking to a friend at my church who's been in the investment business for many years. I asked him for his perspective on the Great Recession and its impact on his peers in the financial industry. He said most investment experts have always thought of themselves as brilliant, and they considered their brilliance to be the reason why they earned so much money for their clients and themselves. But during the long downturn, they discovered that luck and the general economy accounted for a good chunk of their brilliance.

We hate thinking of our own successes this way, don't we? That is why we have a love-hate relationship with grace. We are locked in an all-out conflict between karma and grace. In Michka Assayas's interviews with Bono for his book, *Bono: In Conversation*, the singer/songwriter describes that conflict, asserting that we have "moved out of the realm of karma into one of grace." Assayas then asks Bono for clarification . . .

Bono: At the center of all religions is the idea of karma. You know, what you put out comes back to you: an eye for an eye, a tooth for a tooth, or in physics—in physical laws—every action is met by an equal or an opposite one. . . . And yet, along comes this idea called grace to upend all that "as you reap, so you will sow" stuff. Grace defies reason and logic.

Love interrupts . . . the consequences of your actions, which
in my case is very good news indeed, because I've done a lot
of stupid stuff.

Assayas: I'd be interested to hear that.

Bono: That's between me and God. But I'd be in big trouble if karma was going to finally be my judge. . . . It doesn't
excuse my mistakes, but I'm holding out for grace. I'm holding out that Jesus took my sins onto the Cross, because I
know who I am, and I hope I don't have to depend on my
own religiosity.[4]

A Thorn by Any Other Name

We are all tools. And I don't mean that pejoratively. We are not *a*
tool; we are *the* tool. Who we are—not what we do or what we accomplish or who we know, but we ourselves—is our chief tool for bringing redemptive impact to others in our life. It's not our ideas or our
strategies or our training or our connections or our abilities or our
resources. It's our essence: *we're* the tool.

Edwin Friedman, in his masterwork on leadership, *A Failure of
Nerve*, calls this dynamic "bringing our non-anxious presence"[5]
into every situation. Doing so changes, in turn, the dynamic of every
social system we enter. It's not our words that are game-changers for
people; it's our catalytic presence.

I live in a passionate household. All of us—me, my wife, our
two daughters, and even our dog and cats—have strong personali-
ties. Escalating emotions are the wallpaper of my life. And over the
years, I have discovered—mostly through abysmal and embarrass-
ing failures—that when I throw words at emotion, it's like throwing
gas-soaked kindling on an already roaring fire. But when I instead
bring the strength of my centered presence into the pit, the fire dies
down on its own. It's my non-anxious presence, not my words, that
changes the combustible reaction of escalating emotion.

Our non-anxious presence is our primary tool in our missional life with Christ. But neglected, abused, or broken tools can't do the work they were intended to do. Moreover, tools that suddenly start operating on their own can damage or destroy. For us to be of any benefit, we must recognize our utter dependence on the hand that wields us.

That is the lesson the apostle Paul had to learn. Paul was "caught up into Paradise," where he heard "inexpressible words." But guess what happens next?

> Because of the surpassing greatness of the revelations . . . there was given me a thorn in the flesh, a messenger of Satan to torment me—to keep me from exalting myself! Concerning this I implored the Lord three times that it might leave me. And He has said to me, 'My grace is sufficient for you, for power is perfected in weakness.' Most gladly, therefore, I will rather boast about my weaknesses, so that the power of Christ may dwell in me. Therefore I am well content with weaknesses, with insults, with distresses, with persecutions, with difficulties, for Christ's sake; for when I am weak, then I am strong. (2 Cor. 12:7–10)

Paul had been invited into the counsel of the Holy; he had seen and heard and tasted such great truths that the revelation was almost too much for his Pharisee-of-Pharisees constitution. Now, overwhelmed by the beauty of his experience, he does what all of us do: he starts to believe that the glory he has *tasted* is actually a glory that is ascribed to him. The glory of God splashes on him, and he mistakes "splash" for "fountain." The tool forgets that a hand is wielding it: "Look what I have done," says the hammer, "*all by myself.*" And so, because all of Paul's impact will come down to who he is, not what he does, God jams a thorn in his side—something so frustrating, painful, and irritating that Paul calls it "a messenger of Satan."

The point of all this—the point we so often miss because we know what "thorn" means in our own life, and it's a scary and frustrating reality for us—is that the thorn's purpose is to release our true strength on behalf of others. Paul needs strength to do what he has to do. And the strength we need is the strength Jesus has; it's from Him and in Him, but you and I won't drink from that Well unless we know our own well is dry. The thorn in our side pierces our own well, draining it and leaving us thirsty.

The other day, after I'd been reminded of a thorn in my own side and was lamenting how pitifully my own strength performs under pressure, I whispered a prayer under my breath: *Sorry, Lord. Sorry, sorry, sorry.* I'm well practiced in this basic apology. In the middle of this one, I did something I often do: I asked God if He had anything to say to me, and then I waited.

After a moment or two, I "saw" Psalm 33:13–22 in my mind's eye. So I turned there, and here's what I read:

> The LORD looks down from heaven
> and sees the whole human race.
> From his throne he observes
> all who live on the earth.
> He made their hearts,
> so he understands everything they do.
> The best-equipped army cannot save a king,
> nor is great strength enough to save a warrior.
> *Don't count on your warhorse to give you victory—*
> *for all its strength, it cannot save you.*
>
> But the LORD watches over those who fear him,
> those who rely on his unfailing love.
> He rescues them from death
> and keeps them alive in times of famine.

We put our hope in the LORD.
He is our help and our shield.
In him our hearts rejoice,
    for we trust in his holy name.
Let your unfailing love surround us, LORD,
    for our hope is in you alone.

(NIV, italics mine)

If "warhorse" is just another way of describing our skills, abilities, and gifting, then the psalmist is telling us a hard truth: these things are not to be counted on. Our strengths entice us. We are sorely tempted to depend on our own ability to rise to the occasion rather than throw ourselves on the mercy of Jesus and beg for His strength, His courage, and His excellence. How can we remind ourselves of our need for dependence on Him unless we encounter circumstances that drive us to it?

That's the job of our thorn, isn't it? It's what C. S. Lewis calls a "severe mercy"[6]—severe because it exposes our addiction to our own competence; mercy because it leverages us into a posture of desperate dependence. All of Jesus' best friends were desperate people who understood the currency of grace. And I want to be one of His best friends.

When we are thirsty enough and desperate enough, He has a shot at convincing us to offer our skin in the game—to give with abandon *who we are*, not just what we have.

FOR DISCUSSION OR PERSONAL REFLECTION

- Often our camouflaged refusal to receive grace surfaces when we are complimented by someone. What is your typical response to a compliment, and why do you answer the way you do?

- In the parable of the prodigal son, which of the sons is most like you, and why?
- In C. S. Lewis's *Great Divorce*, the ghost who refuses to receive grace says, "I always done my best and I never done nothing wrong." Like most of us, he thinks of himself as a pretty good person. How would the ghost's description of himself have to change in order for him to accept an invitation to leave hell and enter heaven?
- Tell what this statement means to you: In the kingdom of God, we can ask for anything, but we can buy nothing.
- What is true and what is not true about this statement by Kai Ryssdal: "When all else fails, there's faith"?
- How and why is "desperate dependence" the antidote to a life dominated by the insidious demands of control?
- In what subtle ways have you lived your life as if karma (you get what you deserve) rather than grace (you get what you don't deserve) were true?
- Think about the role of the thorn in Paul's life. What is an equivalent thorn in your own life, and what effect has it had on you?
- What are some of the "warhorses" you trust in your life, and when have you been challenged to put all your hope in God instead of a warhorse?

CHAPTER 3

WILL YOU EMBRACE YOUR TRUE IDENTITY?

The Story of the Caterwauling Canaanite Woman

"If you meet the Jesus of the Gospels, you must redefine what love is, or you won't be able to stand him."

—G. K. Chesterton

On a field trip to Comic-Con, the massive comic subculture conference in San Diego that has morphed into the world's pop culture epicenter, I was reintroduced to the deep craving we all have for an identity we can call our own. With an attendance that would populate a small city (150,000), Comic-Con is both the longest, biggest Halloween party on earth and an in-your-face bacchanal for the creative arts. It's what Johnny Depp would look like if he transmogrified into a conference.

On the first day, I saw a T-shirt slogan that epitomized the geeky, anything-goes vibe at Comic-Con: "Sin Like You Mean It." That sort of bravado is merely a facade that masks the deeper truth about this three-ring circus of the obscure and absurd: Passionate subcultures offer us something bigger, badder, and more beautiful than our everyday life seems to deliver. They give us the "identity bearings" all of us so desperately crave. At Comic-Con, you can dress up like your favorite graphic-novel character and stand in line overnight with thousands of *Twilight*-obsessed fans so you can hang on every word actor Robert Pattinson says, including this gem I heard firsthand: "I don't think I'm particularly funny." *(Not right then you weren't.)* And along the way you track down the identity you've been hunting for your whole life—the unique you that promises meaning and purpose and fulfillment.

As I was walking to the convention center from my hotel one morning, I tried to keep pace with a young guy carrying a bag with the unmistakable conference logo. I stole a longer-than-normal glance at him because he was dressed so remarkably *vanilla* by Comic-Con standards—a simple pair of jeans and a T-shirt. He deviated from this relative blandness in just one telling detail: he was wearing black leather, Batman-like gauntlets that extended from his fingertips to his elbows. In that moment, this guy became my central metaphor for why this gathering of comic book aficionados is important to so many: it both fuels and *marks* their unique identity and offers them a chance to make a statement, no matter how small, about who they are and what they stand for.

People align themselves with a niche or a subculture because *we're all wired to align ourselves with something.* Andy Grossberg, United States editor of *Tripwire Magazine*, affirmed this central truth during a Comic-Con panel discussion: "[Pop culture is] a kind of church, offering people a moral vision, a life mission, and a passionate community of like-minded parishioners."[1]

Jesus understands this need for alignment perfectly. In John 6:35, He says, "I am the Bread of Life. The person who *aligns with me* hungers no more and thirsts no more, ever" (MSG, italics mine).

We have many alignment options, Jesus is saying, but His is the only option that truly *identifies* us.

Is There a There There?

If the skin of "skin in the game" is best translated as "personal risk," then we must have a "personal" to risk. Put another way, my hundred dollars of skin in the game may be a paltry sum, a widow's mite—but it's still *my* paltry sum. And it's the "my" that points to the question of identity.

Until we move toward embracing and living out of our true identity, we labor uphill under the foreboding shadow of the famous Gertrude Stein quote: "There is no there there." Risk implies that we offer up something of substantive value—the hard currency of our core identity. But so many of us worry, in our darkly honest moments, that "there is no there there" where our soul's true identity is supposed to be.

I know firsthand the mechanics of this belief. I was well into adulthood before my secret belief about my own vacant identity was exposed. This part of my life's narrative is so pivotal that I have written about it often in the magazine I edit and the books I write. It has been central in my own journey toward putting my skin in the game, and perhaps my most visceral experience of Jesus fulfilling His proclaimed mission in my life: "He has sent Me to proclaim release to the captives" (Luke 4:18).

Early in my marriage, after a season of escalating conflict with my wife, I left on a business trip wrestling with the reality that divorce might be a real possibility. I was more than haunted by this—I was devastated, panicked, and desperate. I wanted God to reassure me that my worst fears would not come true, but He would not. Instead, as I sat on the floor in a darkened conference room far from home, pouring out my heart to Him, He confronted the empty place where my soul was supposed to be by revealing my true identity. As

I scribbled what I heard in my spirit on a legal pad, God described the "there" of my soul:

> You're a quarterback. You see the field. You're squirming away from the rush to find space to release the ball. You never give up. You have courage in the face of ferocity—in fact, ferocity draws out your courage. You want to score even when the team is too far behind for it to matter. You love the thrill of creating a play in the huddle, under pressure, and spreading the ball around to everyone on the team.
>
> You have no greater feeling than throwing the ball hard to a spot and watching the receiver get to it without breaking stride. In fact, you love it most when the receiver is closely covered and it takes a perfect throw to get it to him. You have the same feeling when you throw a bomb and watch the receiver run under it, or when you tear away from the grasp of a defender, or when you see and feel blood on your elbows or knees and feel alive because of it.
>
> You love to score right after the other team has scored, but you want to do it methodically, first down by first down, right down the field. You love fourth down! You want to win but are satisfied by fighting well.

Of course, this is not a literal description of who I am—I'm not a quarterback in my everyday life (so cross me off your fantasy team). But Jesus is a master in the art of metaphor. So many of his teachings are embedded in metaphor (the branch attached to the vine, the pearl of great price, the treasure in the field, and on and on). And here He's using a metaphor to describe my essence, one that my soul understands deeply—He's unveiling, in the most intimate way possible, what makes me . . . *me*.

And when Jesus relocates our identity by describing us as we really are, He is doing something far more important to our growth than solving our immediate problem. I wanted Him to reassure me that everything was going to be okay with my wife—but He didn't do that, and everything wasn't okay. We separated for three months while we both sought counseling, perspective, and healing. During that three-month "dark night of the soul," I returned again and again to the description of my soul that Jesus gave me in that lonely conference room. I found courage to move through my dark places because my feet walked on the solid footing of my true identity. And this is what Jesus does when He names us—He does not replace our hard path with an easy one—He strengthens our feet to walk the hard path.

In group settings, I often invite people to ask Jesus to do what He did for me—to reveal their true identity. I have them find a space where they can feel alone, then simply ask the same question Jesus first asked His disciples: "Who do you say I am?" (Matt. 16:15 NIV). I tell them to first take authority over their own voice and the voice of God's Enemy—to assert their right to hear only the voice of Jesus, not any other. Then I invite them to ask the question and wait on the Spirit of Jesus to impress an answer on their soul. Sometimes I ask them to open wide their arms as a physical expression of their receptivity. And I always ask them to write what they see or hear or sense. Some people "hear" nothing, for whatever reason, but many take with them something profoundly true that will change forever the way they see themselves. They are found, often for the first time. Afterward, I make sure to remind them to share what they have learned about themselves with someone whose maturity in Christ they trust. Then I encourage them to start revealing to their close and trusted circle of friends what they now know about themselves.

Oswald Chambers says, "God does not tell you what He is going to do—He reveals to you who He is."[2] The corollary to this great truth is that while He is revealing whom He is, He's also revealing *whom we are*. In one of the few times the New Testament records the audible voice of God, after Jesus emerges from the dark waters of His baptism in the river Jordan, the Father bellows, "This is my beloved Son, in whom I am well-pleased." The first words Jesus hears as He is coming up out of the murky river water are words that *identify* Him.

God is far more interested in naming us than fixing us. Rather than fix the source of my great fear, Jesus called forth from the tomb of my heart a true identity, wrapped in grave-clothes, like Lazarus. Woven through His description of me was the essence of who I am— the *skin* of my skin in the game.

I returned home from that trip to a wife who was determined to change the toxic dynamics of our relationship. She asked me to move out, and I left to live with a succession of friends for three months. But the transcendent experience of God "naming" my identity carried me through the hurricane of pain, doubt, and fear that followed. Whatever would happen, I would know the anchoring reality that I had a "there there," and I knew what it was.

Jesus reveals our true identity, helps us to name it, and then shepherds us into fully embracing it. He's pragmatic about this; he calls us into reality, not unreality. There would be no story of the widow's mite if she'd only *made believe* she had a coin to drop in the tithe bucket. That was a real coin clanking into the pile, and it represented the whole scope of her real resources. In that sense, her mite represented her "there there."

Jesus' dogged determination to mark our identity—to make personal risk truly personal for us and then challenge us to stand up for it—helps us make sense of one of the most disturbing and confounding encounters Jesus ever had with anyone, recorded in Matthew 15.

The Dog Who Barked at Jesus

Just out of a tense encounter with the Pharisees in which He has once again confronted their hypocrisy, Jesus withdraws into the wilderness. He needs space. But a local Canaanite woman who hears that He is traveling nearby tracks Him down and begs Him to have mercy on her demon-possessed daughter.

Jesus stares at her in silence. He will not answer her. She is so worked up, caterwauling at Jesus for help, that the disciples beg Jesus to send her away. He tells the woman bluntly that she is not in the privileged class of those He intends to rescue. But she is undaunted, bowing down before Him and pleading, one more time, "Lord, help me!" So Jesus moves from blunt to insulting. "It is not good to take the children's bread and throw it to the dogs," He tells the woman.

What an electric and patently brutal cliff-hanger! How will this desperate, out-of-control woman handle Jesus' brush-off? And how can we possibly explain the Son of God's seemingly coldhearted behavior?

How would we respond to Him if we were in the woman's sandals? We have two choices. We can agree with the story our shame is telling us about ourselves and scurry back from the precipice of epic possibility. Or we can stand with our eyes flashing and our chin jutted and declare that it will no longer matter how others have defined us, no matter how respected or impressive or powerful they may be. *It. Will. No. Longer. Matter.*

So this is how the woman replies:

> "Yes, Lord; but even the dogs feed on the crumbs which fall from their masters' table."

A delighted Jesus responds:

> "O woman, your faith is great; it shall be done for you as you wish."

And it is. The Scripture tells us that the woman's daughter is healed "at once."

This story confronts us with a Jesus who seems determined to offend. While others have asked for and received a healing touch from a kind and compassionate Jesus, the Jesus this woman encounters forces her into a corner and dares her to fight her way out.

Why? If He is good to His core, and He is, then why would He poke at this woman's vulnerability with such casual and uncharacteristic coldness?

She is a Gentile—a Canaanite woman who is descended from Israel's historic enemies and the instigators of its frequent descents into idol-worship. She represents a hated people, and Mark's version of this encounter adds an important detail about her social status: the woman is an "elite" citizen of Greece who is likely used to getting what she wants when she wants it. This makes her response even more impressive, courageous, and ultimately astonishing to Jesus.

Jesus takes risks—invests His skin in the game—like nobody else. And in this volatile interaction with a needy woman, the risk He takes is ripe for being misunderstood by all who saw it firsthand and all who read about it secondhand. All, that is, except for one person—the woman herself. This is a woman who's been discriminated against by Jews her whole life, so to look past an obvious offense and seize hold of what matters most is a chain-rattling lunge toward freedom. Jesus came to set captives free, and that is the result of His interaction with her, no matter how inscrutable His tactics. He's the ultimate pragmatist when it comes to our freedom—Jesus will set off an earthquake in our soul if it will spring loose our prison door.

Winning at Hide-and-Seek

Our God-given identity is revealed when we "live and breathe and move" as if the mirror He holds up to us is actually a true reflection. That mirror is embedded in what His revealed Word says about who we really are, accentuated and specified by our reflection in the Body of Christ (the community of Jesus-followers) and by His direct communication to us in the Spirit. All of this points to our core identity as his born-again, deeply loved sons and daughters. We believe those Scriptures; why, then, do we generally have such trouble pinning down our revealed identity?

For starters, we're bombarded by a cacophony of voices, all competing to define who we are:

- The marketplace would like us to believe that we are primarily a consumer.
- Our boss would like us to believe that we are fundamentally a productive asset whose worth depends on the value of our output.
- Our teachers would like us to believe that we are a problem to be solved, or a challenge to overcome, or even anecdotal proof of their talent and ability.
- Our parents would like us to believe that we are still a dependent child, or a disappointment, or the greatest thing since toast.
- Our music, especially our love songs, would like us to believe that our sexuality dwarfs our other characteristics in importance.
- Our church would like us to believe that mastering another set of biblical principles will put us over the top, Christian-living-wise.
- Our Starbucks barista would like us to believe that we're the sort of person who deserves to add a maple oat nut scone to our order.
- Our fitness instructor, if we have one, would like us to believe that our abs, pecs, and glutes are our defining physical characteristics.
- Our spouse would like us to believe that we are chiefly responsible for his or her happiness and possibly the primary reason why life hasn't turned out the way they expected.

- Our enemies would like us to believe that everything our shame has told us is true.

We could go on and on, but you get the point.

The best way to pinpoint the identity-forming force of the voices that surround you is to study what's going on in your soul after you've had a difficult or dissonance-producing or even uplifting encounter with someone. How is the echo from that encounter describing you?

Not long ago, I led the program for our church's annual family camp. As the speaker, I was to plan three gatherings that would engage and challenge an impossible range of ages, from toddlers to grandparents.

I take lots of risks when I lead people into a deeper understanding of Jesus and biblical truth, using surprising experiences and plenty of interactions to create an environment that's conducive to growth and impact. I never know for sure what will work and what won't. The first two nights went very well; late that Saturday night, my fifteen-year-old daughter looked at me with tears in her eyes and said, "Sometimes I can't believe you're actually my dad." Her awed response seemed too good to be true. Could it be that my daughter was tasting my latent heroism?

But it's a dangerous game to allow the voices of others to have deep access to your identity. I was reminded of this the following morning, when that very same daughter stopped me on the way out of my last, semi-disastrous session and said, "Dad, how could you blow it so badly?" If success whispers our identity, failure screams it with a megaphone.

Of course, there is no end to the voices demanding to define us. And in addition, we have an enemy who is described throughout the Bible, and repeatedly by Jesus, as an opportunistic terrorist bent on killing, stealing, and destroying. In the parable of the wheat and the tares (Matt. 13:24–30), Jesus describes this enemy as one who sneaks into our freshly planted field under cover of darkness and plants weeds right alongside our good crop. Then, to our shock and dismay, the weeds grow up with our wheat. In the parable, Jesus tells us to leave the weed-pulling to Him, because our oafish efforts often uproot the wheat right along with the weeds.

The Enemy has most certainly planted weeds in our life. "Destructive narratives" is another way of describing them. And narratives have clout. In his popular agent-of-change blog, marketing guru and author Seth Godin describes our inexorable attraction to narratives and their power to organize the disparate facts embedded in our experiences:

> Columbus wasn't surrounded by flat-earth believing denialists before he "discovered" America. This was amplified by Washington Irving (!) in a book that was largely invented without much research.
>
> And George Washington didn't cut down the cherry tree and Robin Hood didn't do all those cool tricks in green tights.
>
> The media isn't the one that needs a narrative . . . we do. We need to make sense of what's around us, not just the true things that really happened, but the fictional ones that we know didn't.
>
> All this myth-making reminds us just how strongly wired we are to believe in things that both make sense and feel right. They feel right because of who told us, and when.[3]

Our enemy is an opportunist. He often waits for just the right moment to underscore the destructive narratives we believe about ourselves. One reason those narratives seem so, well, *right* is that we don't recognize the voice behind them—the "who told us" of Godin's observation. We mistake the voice of the Liar for the voice of Truth, because sin has hardwired us to believe the worst about our crop of wheat. The weeds seem truer than the wheat.

In his 1986 masterpiece "The Way It Is," singer/songwriter Bruce Hornsby captures well the moment these destructive narratives are planted in our soul. In the song he's an invisible observer of a line of ragged poor people waiting to get their welfare check. A well-dressed man hurries past the line and sneers at an old woman to get a job.

In Hornsby's streetside vignette, "the way it is" refers to the toxic air of the lies we breathe—ugly narratives that filter into our hearts and kill faith, hope, and love. Telling someone to get a job is not only an insult, it's the tip of a destructive narrative that has the power to crush a life-weary soul. The lies embedded in our destructive narratives purport to tell us the blunt truth about our soul, shorn of romanticism and bankrupt of hope.

> We have an enemy who is determined to plant "truthy" parables and potent narratives in our life that are intended to destroy our true identity.

Life's hardships aren't nearly enough to pry us away from our pursuit of God; indeed, they often draw us closer to him. Our enemy knows this. But he also knows that if he can use those hardships to plant destructive narratives in our life like noxious weeds, then we become his allies in his war against . . . us! When we believe what is not true about ourselves, living out of those narratives as their roots sink deeper, then we do all the heavy lifting of "kill, steal, and destroy."

Jesus says, "If then the light that is in you is darkness, how great is the darkness!" (Matt. 6:23). That is, when the lies that we have embraced as truths about ourselves take root, our darkness is complete. We are both the prisoners and jailers of our soul, playing both roles with equal vigor.

Because we live in a fallen world and we ourselves are fallen, it doesn't take long for the damage of destructive narratives to set in—for the weeds God's enemy has planted to sprout in our soul and grow:

"You'll never amount to anything."

"Your performance is more important than who you are."

"You're damaged goods, and no one will every really want you."

"You're a disappointment to everyone, so you'll never be invited in."

"People will always let you down, so don't open yourself to them."

And in the case of the caterwauling Canaanite woman: "It is not good to take the children's bread and throw it to the dogs."

Hey, wait a minute! That last line was spoken by Jesus! How could He possibly plant something that looks very like a weed—a destructive narrative—in the soul of a woman desperate for His help? How is His voice in this moment any different from the voice of His enemy, who's been sneaking into this woman's wheat field to plant tares her whole life?

The answer, again, lies in Jesus' redemptive passion: "I have come to set captives free."

Hijacking the Voice of Your Enemy

God is shrewder than His enemy in every moment and every circumstance. Here, Jesus' redemptive approach is breathtaking. He intends to pull the tares from the Canaanite woman's narrative wheat field, and He begins by isolating the storyline she has most certainly come to believe about herself, a story of marginalization and racism and diminished humanity. In channeling that narrative, He is calling for her skin in the game, inviting her to yank on the weeds *with* Him. He is, in the vernacular of Joseph, taking what the Enemy "intended [for] harm" and instead "[using] it for good to accomplish . . . the saving of many lives" (Gen. 50:20 NIV).

Identity formation doesn't happen when our circumstances tell us a new and better narrative, which we then embrace; *it happens when we change how we respond to the same narrative that has always been destructive to us.* Jesus will not give this Canaanite woman a truer narrative to embrace until He has enticed her into moving beyond the weed-like lie that has choked her soul, namely, "Grace is for others, not you." Jesus is baiting her. And to His delight and even awe, she responds with a bold (and clever) proclamation: "Yes, Lord; but even the dogs feed on the crumbs which fall from their masters' table."

Jesus translates the dignity and power of the woman's response as "great faith": she is determined to obtain what is true about Jesus no matter what her destructive narrative tells her she deserves. She reaches out to Him and grabs what He has for her. It is a simple four-step response:

1. *Name your destructive narrative*—"I've been told that I am a dog, unworthy of grace."
2. *Renounce your destructive narrative*—"I will not be denied God's goodness based on the false accusations about my identity that I have always believed."
3. *Proclaim the truth about God*—"He is my Master and is well capable of delivering on every promise."
4. *Proclaim the truth about yourself*—"I can receive whatever my Master has for me."

This same redemptive progression is played out in the climactic scene from *The Silver Chair*, the fourth book of C. S. Lewis's classic children's fantasy series, The Chronicles of Narnia. In the story, King Caspian's son, Prince Rilian, has been captured and imprisoned by an evil witch for ten years. As a result of the destructive narratives the witch has planted in his soul, the prince no longer remembers who he really is. He has been seduced into believing the evil witch is good and that his true purpose is to "make myself king over some nation that never did me wrong—murdering their natural lords and holding their throne as a bloody and foreign tyrant."

When his rescuers succeed in freeing him, he is quickly confronted by the witch, who wastes no time repeating the rutted bullet-list that is his destructive narrative. But Rilian, like the Canaanite woman, is determined to change his response to that narrative: "Now that I know myself, I do utterly abhor and renounce it as plain villainy." He follows this naming and renouncing with a proclamation about his father and about himself: "I am the King's son of Narnia, Rilian, the only child of Caspian, Tenth of that name, whom some call Caspian the Seafarer."[4]

The central truth that Lewis speaks through the mouth of Prince Rilian is, *"Now that I know myself. . . ."* In the face of the destructive narratives that have usurped our true identity as beloved children of the King, our skin-in-the-game response is like a sharp stake that we drive firmly into the ground on which we stand, and to which we affix a banner that reads, "Now I know myself."

> Jesus wants to uproot the destructive narratives that have been planted in our life—or more accurately, rewrite them into stories of great beauty. But He requires our skin in the game. We must name our destructive narratives when they surface, renounce them, and embrace the true narrative about who He is and who we are.

The invitation to step out of the shadows of our lies is embedded in every encounter Jesus has with a human being. At the end of Matthew 7, Jesus has just delivered one of the most profound teachings ever uttered, the Sermon on the Mount. Matthew, a tax collector turned disciple and an eyewitness to this feast of truth, observes that "the crowds were amazed at His teaching; for He was teaching them as *one* having authority" (Matt. 7:28-29).

Jesus is suddenly a bona fide sensation, and an enormous crowd follows Him down the mountain. Into this teeming chaos a man who has no business being there—a man who is breaking the law by merely showing up—finds his way to Jesus and bows before him. He is a leper. He is required to shout "Unclean!" to passersby in order to warn them of his presence. But desperate circumstances have fueled his courage, and he says to Jesus, "Lord, if You are willing, You can make me clean."

The man's shame is in the light, and his determination is a declaration: "Yes, my past has shackled me, but I can see freedom in my future, and I'm going to seize my opportunity for it." Jesus then stretches out His hand to touch the man, smashing the man's chains with the sweetest five words he has ever heard: "I am willing; be cleansed" (Matt. 8:2-3).

Of the many lepers on that day who dream of their healing, one has chosen to declare the truth about himself—that he will not be defined by what marginalizes him. Similarly, when the Canaanite woman names, renounces, and proclaims, not just one but two captives are simultaneously set free. The woman's demon-possessed daughter is released from her torment at the very moment when her mother is released into her true identity as a woman of great faith.

Our dreams and our desperation live or die by this question: "Will you embrace your true identity?"

My friend Bob Krulish often signs his emails to me with a kind of call-to-arms—"Live large!" The implication, of course, is that it is possible to "live small," and we need encouragement to live as if our widow's mite actually matters in the world. Why live small if it's in our capacity to live large? We all know why. Living small means operating under the radar. Staying off the target grid. Avoiding the dangerous territory of the Whac-a-Mole board called *risk*.

But freedom is our deepest longing, and we walk out through our prison gates when we discover, then embrace, and then live with passion our "there there."

FOR DISCUSSION OR PERSONAL REFLECTION

- If we're all wired to align ourselves with something, what are a few "alignments" in your life that best reveal who you really are and what you really care about?
- If you transcribed your interior conversations, what are some words you'd find you often use to describe yourself?
- How have voices other than God's influenced whom you have become? What are the primary voices that have shaped you, and how?
- How do you know which identity-shaping voices to listen to and which ones to ignore? How easy or hard is it for you to tune out the latter?
- What destructive narratives are you already aware of in your life, and how have you dealt with them?
- In what ways has God "hijacked the voice of your enemy" in your life?
- Right now, name and renounce a destructive narrative in your life. Then proclaim the truth about God and then the truth about yourself. Having done these things, what was the experience like for you?

CHAPTER 4

WILL YOU OWN WHAT YOU WANT?

The Story of the Crippled Man by the Pool of Bethesda

"Sometimes I think the difference between what we want and what we're afraid of is about the width of an eyelash."

—Jay McInerney

There, next to the sheep gate in Jerusalem, is the notorious little pool the locals call Bethesda. Five covered walkways, or porticoes, lead to the water's edge. And in the shade of these porticoes lies the ugly reality of a wrecked humanity—"a multitude of those who were sick, blind, lame, and withered, [waiting for the moving of the waters; for an angel of the Lord went down at certain seasons into the pool and stirred up the water; whoever then first, after the stirring up of the water, stepped in was made well from whatever disease with which he was afflicted]" (John 5:3–4, brackets in the original).

Among Bethesda's living dead is a man who has made this awful place his home for thirty-eight years. And though everyone in Jerusalem knows exactly why the withered wait and groan there under the porticoes, and though there is no doubt about what they want, Jesus nevertheless asks this man, "Do you wish to get well?"

The crippled man would have every right to take offense—every right to scowl and spit at the man who seems to mock him. Jesus' question is like asking a sky diver if he wants his chute to open—"What, are you trying to offend me, or are you just ignorant?" But instead, the man simply owns what he wants: "Sir, I have no man to put me into the pool when the water is stirred up, but while I am coming, another steps down before me" (John 5:6-7). He's biting his tongue through this response—saying, essentially, "Of course I want to get well, but I can't get someone to help me. Will you help me?" Of the thousand possible ways this man could have responded to Jesus, his "Will you help me?" is the bravest. It's the skin in the game Jesus is looking for.

So, rather than wait to help the man into the pool when the waters stir, Jesus does what the pool cannot: he tells the man to get up off the floor of the portico, grab his pallet, and walk away from a life that is really a death sentence. And the man who owned what he really wanted does just that. He leaves behind a life that orbited around his illness and launches himself into a new solar system.

This man's life has been like a tree growing next to a boulder. It has grown around the hulking impediment of his disability, conforming its shape to its contours. And Jesus is asking the man if he'd like his tree to be replanted in a place where it can spread its branches and assume its natural shape. "Do you wish to get well?" is also "Do you wish to be replanted?"

Amanda Palmer and the Art of Asking Too Much

Our story is, in so many ways, the same as the crippled man's story. Jesus will ask us what we want, and it will take courage to respond with clarity and abandon. It is a vulnerable thing to own what we want. This is why it's rare to run across people, other than criminals, who are comfortable asking for what they want, and even rarer to find those who will receive it wholeheartedly when it's given.

When indie punk rocker and quasi performance artist Amanda Palmer recounts the arc of her oddball career—including her infamous Kickstarter funding campaign that netted $1.2 million for her album *Theatre Is Evil*, making it the most successful crowdsourcing-funded recording project in history—she centers her story around a life philosophy she calls "the art of asking."

Palmer was lead singer of the groundbreaking group The Dresden Dolls before moving on to become the exhibitionistic mistress of ceremonies for the traveling musical circus she calls The Grand Theft Orchestra. But she started out on the streets of Boston as a statue-like mime/busker with painted-white skin, clad in a wedding dress, offering pedestrians a daisy and five seconds of focused eye contact in return for a donation. In that boot camp of vulnerability, Palmer learned to relax as an asker. The experience soon obliterated in her the no-man's zone we've all established between two combatants—our need and our shame. We want things, but our fundamental shame tells us we should not ask for them. This is why the eccentric, the narcissistic, and the pathological are most often the only ones who don't seem to experience the guilty pushback the rest of us feel whenever we ask for things we don't feel we inherently deserve.

On the streets of Boston, Palmer discovered that asking for what she wanted could morph into a sustainable lifestyle. As she interacted with a sea of "lonely people who looked like they hadn't talked to anyone in weeks," she says, "we would sort of fall in love a little bit." From Palmer's perspective, the transaction almost always felt like this: "My eyes would say, 'Thank you. I see you.' Their eyes would say, 'Nobody ever sees me. Thank you.'"

Later in her career as a touring musician, this same transaction played out on a larger scale. Because the costs associated with touring were prohibitive, Palmer and her band often resorted to "couch-surfing"—using social media to ask her fans for a place to crash for the night. Once, she and her band couch-surfed at the home of an impoverished eighteen-year-old girl whose parents were undocumented immigrants from Honduras. The family insisted on sleeping on couches so Palmer and her band could take the beds, and as she fell asleep that night Palmer wondered, "Is this fair?" When she woke the next day, the mother in the family told her, in broken English, "Your music has helped my daughter so much. Thank you for staying here. We're all so grateful." And Palmer thought, "This *is* fair."[1]

Because she found a secret path through the jungle of her fundamental shame—a path called "This *is* fair"—Palmer reframed "asking for what you want" as an act of artistic vulnerability. In her repetitive practice of turning to her fans (and even complete strangers) to give her what she needed, she established a trusting intimacy that continues to fuel her career today monetarily, artistically, emotionally, and even spiritually.

And when Jesus forces the hand of the man by the pool of Bethesda, challenging him to ask for what he wants, He is moving the relationship from a mere transaction to something much more intimate. When the man asks for Jesus' help, he is, in essence, *attaching* himself to Jesus. This is what Jesus means when He proclaims, in John 15:5, "I am the vine, you are the branches; he who abides in Me and I in him, he bears much fruit, for apart from Me you can do nothing." If we can do nothing apart from Him, then *everything* depends on our abiding in Him. And we abide in Him when we own what we want with Him—when we put ourselves on the line to pursue Him with our dreams.

The Blessed Ignorance of Little Children

Intimacy with Jesus will require that we risk enough to ask for what we want, "You do not have because you do not ask," reads

James 4:2. The corollary to that is, "You invest your skin in the game when you summon the courage to ask for what you want." Few of us gravitate to the vulnerability and the risk inherent in asking for what we want.

That is why, when Jesus says, "If you abide in Me, and My words abide in you, ask whatever you wish, and it will be done for you" (John 15:7), his statement is a lot more challenging than it seems at first blush. He's telling us that if we want to experience true intimacy with Him, we'll practice the spiritual discipline of asking.

Little children have perfected the second half of this equation. They almost always ask whatever they wish, and they almost always expect that it will be done for them. Not having experienced profound disappointment in their asking, they're not at all self-conscious about asking for what they want, when they want it, with no consideration for how it might make them appear—because they *expect* that the adults around them can deliver.

A few weeks ago, my ten-year-old daughter came home from school, eager to tell me about her friend's upcoming trip to Hawaii. After describing the happy bullet-list of experiences her friend was about to enjoy in paradise, she asked, as if her request were for a glass of water, "When will we be going to Hawaii?" When my response turned out to be some version of, "That's asking for way too much," I could just about see her synapses sparking, trying to make sense of "too much."

Children don't understand "too much." That is why Jesus says, "Truly I say to you, unless you are converted and become like children, you will not enter the kingdom of heaven" (Matt. 18:3). Asking for too much is the turn of the key into the kingdom of God, which belongs to children. This kind of asking characterizes the life of every single person who was singled out for their "great faith" by Jesus, including the characters we've so far explored in this book, as well as . . .

- Matthew, a notorious sinner who asked Jesus to join him and a bunch of his sinner friends for dinner—and Jesus did (Matt. 9).
- Peter, who asked Jesus to make it possible for him to walk on water—and Jesus did (Matt. 14).
- A man living with the death sentence of leprosy, who asked Jesus to cure him—and Jesus did (Matt. 8).
- The centurion who asked Jesus to heal his paralyzed servant by "just say[ing] the word"—and Jesus did (Matt. 8).
- The men who lowered their friend through the roof of a meeting place so they could ask Jesus to heal him (Mark 2).
- Martha, who asked Jesus to raise her dead brother Lazarus from the dead (John 11).
- Blind Bartimaeus, who repeatedly cried to Jesus for mercy and then requested, "Rabbi, I want to see" (Mark 10 NIV).
- The men who brought their deaf and dumb friend to Jesus, begging Him to heal the man—and Jesus did (Mark 7).

Faith is our determined response to the character and capability of Jesus. My daughter asks for way too much because she believes I can do and provide anything for her. *Anything*. Because she is a child, she has not yet learned that my character and capability are limited resources. (Just wait, dear.) But those limitations are not true of Jesus. And when we take the risk of asking way too much of Him, we behave like the little children He urges us to become. We are making a statement about our belief in His character and capability and then rolling the dice on it.

Practicing Our Accidental Buddhism

Most of us are closet Buddhists. We believe the path to happiness requires a kind of death to our deepest wants, because those wants are also responsible for our deepest pain and suffering.

In *The Journey of Desire*, author John Eldredge writes, "Desire is the source of our most noble aspirations and our deepest sorrows. The pleasure and the pain go together; indeed, they emanate from the same region in our hearts. We cannot live without the yearning, and yet the yearning sets us up for disappointment—sometimes deep and devastating disappointment."[2]

In answer to this dilemma, Buddhism prescribes *suppressed desire* as the cure to all our ills: if you give up on your wants, you will be free from their tyranny. This exchange of risk for safety seems prudent—and it appears to work for millions, including many followers of Christ who have no idea that their solution to the pain of unmet desire is more Buddhist than gospel.

To understand the genesis and structure of our accidental Buddhism, it helps to know how the seeds of Buddhist thought and practice were sown more than two millennia ago.

Buddhism is a pre-Christian movement founded by Prince Siddhartha Gautama ("The Buddha") 2,500 years ago. Gautama's parents, the king and queen of Kapilavastu, gave their son every luxury. He married when he was sixteen, and his father built the young couple three palaces so they would have no pretext for pursuing unmet wants outside of his kingdom. But Gautama grew more and more restless in his life of ease, so he traveled from his palaces to experience the wider world. There he found sickness, injury, and death all around him, and it shattered him. He thought, "How can I enjoy a life of pleasure when there is so much suffering in the world?"

On his fourth trip to the outside world, he ran into a monk who'd given up all his possessions to seek an end to suffering in the world. The young man decided that this would also be his own life's quest. Gautama renounced his life of luxury and all of his family to pursue a cure to the world's unhappiness. He cut off his hair, wore ragged clothing, and ate roots, leaves, and fruit. But after six years of wandering from place to place, living the life of an ascetic, he decided that neither extreme—neither luxury nor poverty—offered a miracle cure for suffering.

Then, in a season of solitary meditation, he wrestled his way to "enlightenment," ultimately propagating a set of teachings he called the *Dharma*, which include his description of "four noble truths." Truths two and three of the *Dharma* explain the cause of suffering and its cure. Our problem, said Gautama, is that we want too much. Our greed causes us to live in a constant state of perceived deprivation: "Once children have had a taste of candy, they want more. When they can't have it, they get upset. Even if children get all the candy they want, they soon get tired of it and want something else. Although, they get a stomachache from eating too much candy, they still want more. The things people want most cause them the most suffering."[3]

The solution to this problem, says Gautama, is that we must make our way toward *nirvana*, which he describes as "the extinction of desire." In Buddhist philosophy, the obliteration of our driving desires is the only way we can end our suffering. Removing want as a human characteristic is the pathway to happiness. It's a simple equation: remove the impetus of desire and, sure, we're capitulating to a life of quiet desperation, but we're also shielding ourselves from the shattering we experience when our wants go unnoticed and unmet.

My wife and I were engaged three times. Do the math and you'll realize that we had two painful dis-engagements. The second time when Bev broke off our relationship, just a few months before our wedding, the pain was so overwhelming that I retreated into an unmarked dark cave somewhere in my soul's interior, where I could divorce myself from desire and hide out. And in that dark place, I made a vow that I believed would keep me from ever entering that cave again: "I will never, ever allow my heart to hope in the restoration of my relationship with Bev again. I will put a bullet through the head of my deepest desire."

I made good on my Buddhist-style vow. For six months I could've put any monk to shame. Whenever I saw Bev at church or at gatherings of mutual friends, and the desire I thought I had killed stirred to life, I pulled the trigger and killed it all over again. I determined that, over time, my desire would soon be so full of bullet holes that there would be nothing left to stir.

But six months into my "Buddhist" life, at a wedding reception for a friend, Bev sought me out to ask a simple question: "I miss you. Do you think we could meet to talk?" I pulled my figurative gun from its holster one more time and put my finger on the trigger. But this time, I couldn't pull it. I just couldn't.

A year later we married. That was twenty-four years ago.

Desire in my life has brought me back to the dark cave of pain and suffering many times since I laid down my "gun." But that's okay, because the life philosophy advocated by Buddhism is, in the end, a form of cowardice. We are not to fear death, unless it's the death of our desires.

In a sermon that was later included in a book called *The Weight of Glory and Other Addresses*, the great apologist C. S. Lewis said: "If we consider the unblushing promises of reward and the staggering nature of the rewards promised in the Gospels, it would seem that Our Lord finds our desires, not too strong, but too weak. We are half-hearted creatures, fooling about with drink and sex and ambition when infinite joy is offered us, like an ignorant child who wants to go on making mud pies in a slum because he cannot imagine what is meant by the offer of a holiday at the sea. We are far too easily pleased."[4]

Our life runs through, not around, the valley of the shadow of death. Jesus said, "Truly, truly, I say to you, unless a grain of wheat falls into the earth and dies, it remains alone; but if it dies, it bears much fruit" (John 12:24). We bear much fruit when we die to our demand for certainty. When we ask for what we want, we will experience pain. That's the price we pay when we offer our skin in the game. But what happens in our soul when we risk our skin anyway, despite the certainty of suffering—that's what "astonishes" God. He respects courage and persistence.

The Parable of the Persistent Widow

One of the mysteries of the kingdom of God that Jesus took pains to reveal is this: *Our persistence in asking for what we want matters to God.*

One day Jesus told his disciples a story to show that they should always pray and never give up. "There was a judge in a certain city," he said, "who neither feared God nor cared about people. A widow of that city came to him repeatedly, saying, 'Give me justice in this dispute with my enemy.' The judge ignored her for a while, but finally he said to himself, 'I don't fear God or care about people, but this woman is driving me crazy. I'm going to see that she gets justice, because she is wearing me out with her constant requests!'"

Then the Lord said, "Learn a lesson from this unjust judge. Even he rendered a just decision in the end. So don't you think God will surely give justice to his chosen people who cry out to him day and night? Will he keep putting them off? I tell you, he will grant justice to them quickly! But when the Son of Man returns, how many will he find on the earth who have faith?" (Luke 18:1–8 NLT)

When we "drive God crazy" with our persistence, He translates this as an investment of our skin in the game. And that's what He's looking for. He will not do *for* us what He can do *with* us. He is not holding back because He lacks compassion for our circumstances; rather, He is, as author William Paul Young asserts, "respecting His creation more than we do."[5] Young means that God, unlike every human being, never allows himself to relate codependently.

Marriage and family therapist Tina Tessina says, "Codependency, by definition, means making the relationship more important to you than you are to yourself. It's kind of a weird phrase, and it doesn't sound like it means a one-sided relationship. But that's what it is. It means you're trying to make the relationship work with someone else who's not."[6] Those of us who are codependent often make choices for others in our life because we respect their choices more than our own. We can't bear the pain of giving them the freedom to fail—or even to choose paths we don't respect.

But God is never disrespectful of us. That is why He wants us to ask Him for the things we desire, because it would be demeaning to us if He overruled our freedom to choose and our responsibility to ask, thus making it a one-sided relationship.

There is dignity in work. This truth is central to how God created us: "Then God said, 'Let Us make man in Our image, according to Our likeness; and let them *rule over* the fish of the sea and over the birds of the sky and over the cattle and over all the earth, and over every creeping thing that creeps on the earth'" (Gen. 1:26, italics mine). Our DNA is embedded with the expectation and the dignity of "ruling over," and desire, rightly ordered, is integral to our rulership. We are living in the kingdom of God not by following the Buddhist path that skirts desire, but by taking the path that plunges us into the very heart of desire.

FOR DISCUSSION OR PERSONAL REFLECTION

- When was the last time you asked for something you didn't really deserve? What thoughts and emotions did you experience then and since then?
- Why do so few of us live the way Amanda Palmer has learned to live? What keeps us from practicing "the art of asking"?
- Why does asking for what we want from God move our relationship with Him to a greater depth of intimacy?

- When have you "asked too much" of God, and what happened as a result?
- How have you practiced "closet Buddhism" in your life, suppressing your desires in order to avoid disappointment?
- God refuses to be codependent in His relationship with us; He will not make His relationship with us more important than He is to Himself. How have you seen evidence of this truth in your relationship with Him?

CHAPTER 5

WILL YOU CONFRONT YOUR FEARS?

The Story of the Disciples and the Water-Walking Ghost

"A man that flies from his fear may find that he has only taken a shortcut to meet it."

—J. R. R. Tolkien

Jesus has just miraculously fed more than five thousand people on a barren hillside. Now the curious crowd has morphed into a frenzied mob that intends to forcibly install Him as king. What does Jesus do? What He so often does—He withdraws to the wilderness to be by Himself.

The disciples wait for Him by the shores of the Sea of Galilee for hours, but it is getting dark. They can stay no longer if they hope to cross the sea to Capernaum. So off they go in their boat without Jesus.

They have rowed three or four miles into a gathering storm. Out of the gloom comes Jesus, walking on the water toward them.

Nothing in their experience has even remotely prepared them for such a spectacle. Their first, terrified thought is that it must be a ghost—and it's heading in their direction. They're trapped in a boat in the middle of the sea on a stormy night, scared out of their wits, watching the unmistakable figure of a man walking toward them over the choppy water.

Is Jesus, on this night, intending to scare them? He is not only God; He is also man, and He well understands what a man might feel if he sees a person walking on the sea in the middle of a storm in the middle of the night. So He identifies Himself and asks His disciples to let Him in the boat—to believe in who He is. And they do. John understates the tipping point: "So they were willing to receive Him into the boat" (John 6:21). "Willing to receive" means they had to choose to move into and through their fears. How many "ghosts" have you invited into your boat? And once they do, they arrive at their destination "immediately."

Jesus not only uses metaphors to teach, but He also *lives* His metaphors—and the message of the metaphor, silently expressed by what He does here on the stormy Sea of Galilee, is this: *"Confront your fears and invite Me in, and I will give you your destination."*

Five summers ago, my daughter Lucy, ten at the time, asked if she could attend a week-long summer camp in the mountains. It was her first such adventure, and the whole prospect of it was entirely frightening to my wife, who had never been to camp when she was little. Seven straight days with no contact between Lucy and us? No way, my wife decided. On the surface, she was afraid of what our daughter would experience away from us for the first time. But, in truth, Bev was more afraid that she, herself, wouldn't be able to endure the separation well—sleepaway camp represented a threat to her intimacy with Lucy, because it was her first act of letting go.

But Lucy was so clearly ready and eager for this experience, and she revisited her request in such an honest and respectful way, that I urged my wife to reconsider. Finally, Bev saw that her fears were her problem, not our daughter's. So we dropped Lucy off at camp, where she unrolled her sleeping bag in a huge teepee that she would share with six strangers (and some very aggressive squirrels) for the rest of the week.

Bev's tears carried us all the way down the hills back to Denver. It was a significant rite of passage for our family. Bev and Lucy both faced their fears that week. And that means that, in their own ways, both of them put their skin in the game. Lucy let go of her home's moorings and set out into a foreign world where she knew no one. Bev let go of her daughter for the first time.

It is the letting go in the face of fear that is so remarkable and so astonishing—and even miraculous.

It struck me then, and strikes me more deeply now, that Lucy's sleepaway camp experience is a lot like the ghostly Jesus walking on the water toward His frightened disciples. Whatever His intentions, we can be certain of one thing: His choice to stroll past their boat on the water, in the middle of an already frightening night, produced something like panic in His disciples—many of whom were seasoned fishermen who'd weathered plenty of stormy nights on the sea. *Jesus was not merely entering into their fear—He was producing it.*

Because of its ability to threaten and expose our trust issues, fear has an unmatched capacity to drag what we hide in the dark into the blinding light. Fear highlights our core beliefs about ourselves, others, and God. Fear, and how we lean into it (or not), has the leveraging power to transform us.

Our experience in releasing our daughter into the unknown, in the face of Bev's fears, is a parable that describes the "graduated" way Jesus moves in our life as we move toward Him. The closer we get to Him and the more we mature in Him, the more determined He is to send us to sleepaway camp.

Jesus wants to bring our fears to the surface, where they become a visceral reality. This paves the way for us, like the panicked disciples huddled in the boat, to invite Him into our raw need. Jesus wants us to face our inherent fears and learn to relate to Him in an increasing stance of dependent independence—an oxymoron that could be translated as "maturing in Christ."

Parenting itself is a metaphor for this. It was necessary for both Bev and Lucy that Lucy go away to camp. No parent would be satisfied with a healthy teenager who acts like a toddler or with an adult who acts like a teenager. The poet, preacher, and author George MacDonald writes, "What father is not pleased with the first tottering attempts of his little one to walk? What father would be satisfied with anything but the manly step of a full-grown son?"[1]

We intrinsically understand that with maturity comes greater responsibility and greater freedom. Lucy needed to go away so she could step into herself a little more, and she also needed to go away in order to surface my wife's fear, which also revealed Bev's own issues with trust. Our impact for the kingdom of God is directly tied to the way we embrace—or don't embrace—Jesus' changing expectations of us as we move closer to Him. He will scare the snot out of us, then ask if He can sit with us in our boat, and finally take us to our destination once it is no longer the focus.

The Universality of "Be Safe!"

By age eighteen, the average young person in Western culture has witnessed more than 200,000 violent acts on television. A good number of those TV scenes portray what actually happens in real life. More than four million adolescents in the United States, for example, have been victims of a serious physical assault, and nine million have witnessed violence firsthand during their lifetimes. One in twelve has been threatened with or injured by a weapon.[2] Violence and the fear it fuels saturate our culture.

In the fifteen seconds between the two blasts in the 2013 Boston Marathon terrorist bombings, three people—one of them an eight-year-old boy—suffered mortal wounds, and 264 people suffered serious injury. Whether you were an octogenarian lying in bed at a nursing home or a toddler playing in front of the TV at home, you were conscripted into the ranks of eyewitnesses.

Two days after the bombings, *Morning Edition* reporter Alix Spiegel interviewed Jeff Greenberg, a psychologist at the University of Arizona who studies how people respond to events that force them to confront their own fears.[3] Greenberg says that we follow a kind of psychological script when we see something that scares us:

Our kneejerk reaction is horror: *"I can't believe this is happening."*

1. We quickly assess our personal vulnerability: "Could this terrible thing happen to me?"
2. We bias our conclusion in a way that denies our vulnerability: "I live in Colorado, not Boston. There are no terrorists here."
3. We do what we can to reassert our illusion of control over the chaos that threatens to invade our life: "We should pay more attention to security issues in our city and increase our vigilance."

After this initial progression, the event migrates from our conscious to our unconscious mind. Greenberg says, "The thoughts of our mortality tend to linger outside of our conscious attention but still affect us."[4] After the 9/11 terrorist attacks in New York, Pennsylvania, and Washington, DC, Greenberg and his colleagues gave a wide range of people incomplete "word stems" and asked them to finish the words. "You could fill it out with a death-related word or a non-death-related word—so, for example, coff- could be either 'coffee' or 'coffin,'" he says. For many months after the attacks, people were significantly more likely to choose "coffin" than "coffee."

Greenberg adds, "When death is percolating close to consciousness, people become more 'us vs. them'—they become defensive of their belief system, positive toward those they identify with and more negative to those who espouse a different belief system."[5] This is a protective instinct that unconsciously pushes threats away. As the perceived threats in our world increase, so do our fears, and our protective impulse builds momentum.

I met with a friend for lunch, and as we got ready to leave, our waitress stopped, lowered her voice for impact, and then said, "Be safe!" As she turned on her heel, I remarked to my friend, "Isn't that a strange way to say goodbye!" Of course, we're used to it in our culture. "Be safe" is an almost universally accepted alternative for "goodbye." When did "Be safe" become our best farewell? Probably since Columbine, 9/11, AIDS, Virginia Tech, drunk drivers, drug overdoses, alcohol poisonings, online predators, tsunamis, killer hurricanes, killer tornadoes, Sandy Hook, and marathon bombings. Our culture is brimming with dangers, even though we experience very few of them personally. But our increasing protective momentum requires us to work ever harder to reassert our "illusion of control." We want better security, stiffer criminal penalties, higher walls, and lots more control over our environment.

But "Be safe" is not a kingdom of God response to fear. Jesus urged His followers to risk in the face of pervasive or even sudden fear—to put their skin in the game. In fact, the ways he said hello and goodbye often conveyed just the opposite of "Be safe":

"Do not fear" (Luke 5:10).
"Be a testimony to me" (Luke 5:14, my paraphrase).
"Go in peace" (Luke 8:48).
"Take nothing for your journey" (Luke 9:3).
"Proclaim the kingdom of God" (Luke 9:60).
"Be awake and alert!" (Luke 21:36, my paraphrase).

On the stormy Sea of Galilee, after Jesus has scared the wits out of His disciples, He challenges them to move *into* their fear rather than away from it. It's no stretch to say that Jesus is likelier to wave goodbye with a hearty "Be dangerous!" than a cautious "Be safe!" *Wild at Heart* author John Eldredge once told me that we've erred in telling Christian boys that their highest calling is to be nice when we should be telling them to be dangerous for God.[6] So true. But our experience of fear has funneled us toward learned responses that, once again, are not characteristic of little children.

The Little Albert Experiment

In 1920, Johns Hopkins University psychologist John B. Watson published a research paper that came to be known as "The Little Albert Experiment." In it, he introduced the concept of "fear conditioning"—essentially, that we develop fears as a learned response to outside stimulus. Under now dubious circumstances, Watson convinced a nurse who worked at the university's hospital to offer her nine-month-old boy (nicknamed Albert for the study) as a guinea pig for Watson's experiments with fear conditioning.

Watson and his assistant exposed Albert to his first-ever encounters with a white rabbit, a rat, a dog, a monkey, masks with and without hair, cotton wool, and burning newspapers. In his initial exposures, Albert showed no fear toward any of these stimuli. But later, whenever he touched a rat to play with it, Watson made a sudden and loud sound behind him. The baby reacted in fear, crying until he was soothed.

After several rounds of this treatment, the researchers placed a rat near Albert but made no loud sounds. Immediately (and predictably), Albert showed great distress as soon as the rat appeared in the room. He cried, turned away from the rat, and tried to escape. Fear, concluded Watson, is not inherent; it is a learned response that may or may not be congruent with a perceived threat's ability to actually harm us.

This is, essentially, how we develop phobias: our experience of a traumatic event morphs into a conditioned response that is nearly impossible to change. In the case of little Albert, Watson intended to "de-condition" the baby before he left the study, but that never happened. The whole episode was, at the very least, abusive and scandalous.

During one of Watson's many post-study lectures on fear conditioning, a young graduate student named Mary Cover Jones was motivated to explore de-conditioning strategies for people who had developed autonomic fear responses to certain stimulus. Her most successful strategy was something she called "direct conditioning." For example, she gave a three-year-old boy with a preexisting fear of white rabbits a portion of his favorite food every time such a rabbit was introduced into his presence. The boy was eventually able to tolerate the rabbit—to touch it without fear—because its association with something deeply positive overruled its association with fear.

Woven through Jones's discovery is an exegesis of the disciples' encounter with Jesus on the Sea of Galilee. First, He introduces a universal fear (a ghost-like man walking on the water toward their boat), then invites his friends to push through their fear and open themselves to His presence. He drags their fear to the surface, then offers Himself as a "favorite food" to recondition them. He wants them to associate His presence alone, not a change in their circumstances, with safety. It is still night. It is still stormy. And Jesus still looks like a ghost on the water. But once He is inside the boat, His disciples know it is clearly Him, not an apparition.

Fear is the playing field for dependent faith. Dependence will motivate us to risk our skin in the game when fear is dragging us back from the precipice. The end game here is Jesus moving us toward dependence on His person—and dependent-on-Jesus people are always a force to contend with, because they are connected to a power and authority that is much greater than their own.

No One Laughs at God in a Hospital

Singer/songwriter Regina Spektor captures the dynamic outcome of a dependent relationship with God in her brilliant song "Laughing With," from the *Far* album. The song is an exploration of our relationship with God when we are at our most desperate—Spektor lists the lonely, scary, and daunting life experiences that naturally draw us into a raw dependence on God, no matter how we behave in the rest of our life. Spektor says we never laugh at God when we're confined to a hospital bed or when we're in the heat of war or in the midst of starvation or cold or poverty. And we don't laugh at God when a policeman knocks on our door and says, "We got some bad news, sir," or when we're caught up in a famine or decimated by fire or undone by a flood.

Spektor nails it. No one is laughing at God when they actually *need* Him. And our fears surface our need for God. But admitting that need is considered an admission of crippling weakness in our culture. Skeptics, atheists, and those who are uncomfortable going all-in with Jesus believe, to varying degrees, that faith in God is a crutch, indicative of a kind of pansy-weakness that is intolerable to people living in a make-it-happen culture. Who can afford a dependent posture in a world that demands toughness and strength?

When NFL offensive lineman Jonathan Martin of the Miami Dolphins abruptly left the team in the middle of the 2013 season because, he alleged, noted bad-boy lineman Richie Incognito had mercilessly bullied him, the biggest surprise was the backlash against Martin. Many in the sports community and the culture at large accused Martin of being too soft to play in the NFL. For example, when *Denver Post* columnist Benjamin Hochman asked Bronco defensive lineman Terrence Knighton whether he'd want Martin on his team, Martin bluntly replied, "He'd have a hard time finding friends in here. There are no soft players in this locker room, and there's nobody who doesn't stand up for themselves as a man."[7]

We live by a simple dog-eat-dog ethic: Dependence of any kind is an unaffordable weakness. And there may be some truth to that, especially when it comes to chemical and relational dependencies. But not when it comes to God. All of us will, at some point, be compelled to stop laughing at God, whether in this life or the next. There are circumstances in which dependence on God seems the perfectly rational response, and at those times, we experience a kind of clarity that afterward is easy to brush off as just fear-induced desperation. But that desperation, not our everyday independence, is what whispers the truth to us: that our dependence on God, sometimes driven by fear, shows us the path to life.

The agonizing and inspiring story of nineteenth-century lawyer and businessman Horatio G. Spafford has been largely forgotten, but in its day, it was well-known, and for good reason. Spafford and his wife, Anna, were close friends of D. L. Moody, the renowned evangelist and preacher. After a string of financial successes, the Spaffords were dragged into a sequence of tragedies that left no pretext for "laughing at God." First, their four-year-old son died of scarlet fever. The following year, the Great Chicago Fire of 1871 wiped out all of the Spafford's real estate holdings.

Horatio decided it was time for the family to get out of Chicago for an extended time of rest and recuperation in England. With plans to connect with Moody on his European evangelistic campaign, the Spaffords traveled with their four daughters to New York, where they planned to catch the French steamer *Ville du Havre* for a trip across the Atlantic. But just before they set sail, a last-minute business development forced Horatio to delay his own departure. He persuaded his family to go as planned and promised to catch up with them soon.

Nine days later, Spafford's wife sent him a telegram from Wales that read, "Saved alone." The *Ville du Havre* had collided with a Scottish clipper called the *Loch Earn* and sunk to the bottom of the

Atlantic, killing 226 passengers and crew. Anna Spafford clung to her daughters, but the vortex created by the sinking ship tore them from her arms. Miraculously, debris from the wreck floated under Anna's unconscious head, saving her from drowning.

After her rescue, Anna was gripped by despair. But into this horror the voice of God spoke to her: "You were spared for a purpose."

Horatio boarded the next ship out of New York to join his shattered wife. As his ship passed over the exact location where the *Ville du Havre* sank, Horatio retreated to his cabin and penned these raw and soaring lyrics:

> When peace, like a river, attendeth my way
> When sorrows like sea billows roll
> Whatever my lot, Thou hast taught me to say
> It is well, it is well, with my soul.
>
> Though Satan should buffet, though trials should come
> Let this blest assurance control
> That Christ hath regarded my helpless estate
> And hath shed His own blood for my soul.
>
> My sin—oh, the bliss of this glorious thought!—
> My sin, not in part but the whole
> Is nailed to the cross, and I bear it no more.
> Praise the Lord, praise the Lord, O my soul![8]

There is no more unlikely association than Regina Spektor and Horatio G. Spafford, but they are speaking a kindred poetry. The only people who can say, "It is well with my soul," are those who've been driven into desperate dependence on Jesus—those for whom the truth of His redemption, mercy, and love are not just "biblical principles" but water to a dying man in the desert.

The Divine Vintner

In the wine column of the *Washington Post*, wine expert Ben Giliberti once explained the fundamental difference between truly superior wines and so-called bulk vintages:

> Great wines come from low-yielding vineyards planted in marginal climates on the poorest soils. Though hard on the vines, these tough conditions are good for the wine, because vines that are stressed must work harder to produce fruit, which leads to fewer but more concentrated and flavorful grapes. By contrast, the vines used for bulk wines have it easy. They are planted in the fertile soils in ideal climates of regions such as California's Central Valley. Such regions are great for producing tons of grapes to fill up the bulk fermentation tanks, but not at all great for producing the complex, intense flavors needed to make great wine, because the vines are not stressed and the yields are way too high."[9]

The kinds of "tough conditions" that produce great wine also produce martyrs and saints and, if we will lean into our fears and offer our skin in the game, "beautiful messes" like you and me. Fearful circumstances give us windows of opportunity to trade dependence on our own resources for the "riches of His grace."

In 2 Corinthians 4:7-10, Paul describes this transforming reality like this: "We have this treasure in earthen vessels, so that the surpassing greatness of the power will be of God and not from ourselves; we are afflicted in every way, but not crushed; perplexed, but not despairing; persecuted, but not forsaken; struck down, but not destroyed; always carrying about in the body the dying of Jesus, so that the life of Jesus also may be manifested in our body."

We grow not from our easy experiences but from our challenging ones. One summer, when I served as a counselor to at-risk kids at a

Christian camp for low-income, urban teenagers, I was thrown into an almost perpetual state of fear and dependence on God. At one point, I discovered that one of my kids had stolen a butcher knife from the camp kitchen and had hidden it in our cabin, intending to murder me in my sleep. Many of these kids were gang-affiliated, and some of them were deeply disturbed because of their horrific life circumstances. One guy seemed oppressed by demonic influences. And for no particular reason, that guy decided it would be helpful if I was dead. Just by chance, on the day he intended to use the knife on me, I accidentally opened a door to his hiding place and discovered it.

Midstream in my experience, I was far too occupied with maintaining my sanity to notice whether I was growing. But on my first two-day break, I drove into town and walked for hours in silence, and during that time, I experienced God quietly, gently reordering the tectonic plates of my life. He was taking the raw material of my sometimes panicky attempts to reach those desperate kids and forming in me a new capacity for loving others. In my weakness, He'd made me strong.

I'm sure you could say something very similar. If you were to describe the turning points in your own journey with God—those undeniable growth spurts that now form the foundation of your identity—you would almost surely describe a fearful experience followed by some kind of deeper attachment to God. That is the counterintuitive result when, facing our fears, we invite Jesus to step off of the thrashing waves and into our boat. That's when we discover He is no ghost, but real, present, and utterly trustworthy for those who depend on Him.

FOR DISCUSSION OR PERSONAL REFLECTION

- I've said Jesus *intended* to scare the disciples when he walked toward them across the water on that "dark and stormy night."

How does that thought challenge your view of Him—or perhaps undergird it?

- What have been the significant fears you've had to deal with in your life, and how have they impacted your relationships with others and with God?
- How has God brought beauty out of the ugliness of your fears?
- In our culture, safety is one of our top concerns. What are the positives and negatives of that emphasis?
- If the only way to confront and overcome our fears is direct conditioning, what implications does that have for your life?
- Why is the idea behind Regina Spektor's song "Laughing With" true?
- When and why have you been desperately dependent upon God in your life, and how did that experience change you?

CHAPTER 6

WILL YOU RISK?

The Story of the Mud-Smeared Man, Blind from Birth

"Many people are afraid to fail, so they don't try. They may dream, talk, and even plan, but they don't take that critical step of putting their money and their effort on the line. To succeed in business, you must take risks. Even if you fail, that's how you learn. There has never been, and will never be, an Olympic skater who didn't fall on the ice."

—Donald Trump

It doesn't take a theologian or even an off-the-shelf follower of Jesus to underscore the necessity of risk in a life well lived. Case in point: the notorious real estate magnate Donald Trump. Both celebrated and ridiculed, Trump emerged from near-bankruptcy in the mid-1980s to become a high-profile evangelist for risk-taking. We expect that sort of thing from an entrepreneur, but Jesus makes it clear that taking risks is just as crucial for all of us non-Trumps.

Risk, like faith, is a morally neutral force; it can be either a powerfully good thing or a powerfully bad thing, depending on its focus. I've had friends who left the safety of a paycheck and company-paid benefits for the stark uncertainty of starting their own business, and I've watched their risk turn into a personal and professional train wreck. But I also know people who've launched themselves into a freelance career that succeeded beyond their wildest dreams. Risk has no inherent life-giving properties and no guaranteed upside—unless it's a risk that's leading us to Jesus.

The Sanity of His Insanity

Jesus has, once again, offended the Pharisees and teachers of the law so profoundly that they intend to stone him to death. He has just pulled the pin on this little grenade: "You are of *your* father the devil, and you want to do the desires of your father. He was a murderer from the beginning, and does not stand in the truth because there is no truth in him" (John 8:44). John records what happens next with elegant simplicity: "Jesus hid Himself and went out of the temple." It is no doubt the sort of thrilling escape that is worthy of an Ian Fleming storyline, but John reduces it to the bare facts.

That's the prequel to the drama that is about to unfold. Likely breathless from his escape, Jesus comes across a man who is blind from birth (John 9). When the disciples catch up to Jesus, they ask the kind of question that is still common today: "Rabbi, who sinned, this man or his parents, that he would be born blind?" They want to know why bad things happen to good people. It's a conundrum fundamental to human beings everywhere in every culture.

"It was neither that this man sinned, nor his parents," Jesus replies, "but it was so that the works of God might be displayed in him." Then, without permission or hesitation—or, it has to be said, apparent rationality—the Master spits on the ground, fashions a little clay, then smears it all over the man's eyes and face.

As shocking as all of this must have been for a blind man who's suddenly been sucked into a big moment, the next words out of Jesus' mouth must have seemed no less astonishing: "Go, wash in the pool of Siloam" (John 9:1–7).

The pool is on the other side of town, a long trek away. And this man has just been told to walk there on his own. Still blind, his eyes smeared with spit and mud, he's to make his way to a pool where he can wash his face. If he can find the place.

What's the point?

Why would Jesus ask this man to do something that will so obviously require him to take a great risk?

Why, when He has healed multitudes with a simple touch, does Jesus ask the man to jump through hoops in order to find his freedom?

It makes no sense—unless risk is what Jesus wants to draw out of the man.

Jesus is directly connecting risk to displaying the works of God. The man's skin in the game sets the stage for God to be known and worshiped.

The blind man is used to poor treatment, and getting clay smeared in his eyes smacks of same-old, same-old. So why should he obey Jesus' bizarre instructions, after an equally bizarre and inexplicable act of apparent disrespect? We don't know the calculus going on inside the man's head, but we do know his response. He accepts Jesus' challenge and finds his way to the pool of Siloam, where he washes the clay from his eyes—and then runs back through town to declare the impossible: He can see! For the first time in his life, he can see!

We may not like the hard edge of risk, but Jesus requires it of those who would wash away their blindness.

It's important to consider the dimensions of the man's risk—and our own, because our courage is proportionate to its impediments. Like the man born blind, we've heard the Accuser's voice our whole life, planting his lies in our soul.

On a men's retreat a couple of years ago, my friend Bob Krulish asked a group of sixty gathered in a mountain auditorium to answer this simple question: "What's one lie you are right now believing about yourself?" Here's a sampler of their anonymous responses:

I'm not really desired by my wife.
I'm not enough (listed multiple times).
I always feel like a failure.
If you really knew me, you'd reject me (listed multiple times).
I'm not worthy or capable of success.
I'm invisible.
I'm inadequate.
My life isn't worth much or special.
I'm dirty.
I'm a loser.
I can't do it.
I don't have what it takes
I can do it all by myself—don't need others.
There is something wrong with me.[1]

What about the man born blind, with mud smeared on his weathered face? His own interior collection of lies may well be legion—a toxic stew of the entire bulleted list. But he chooses to risk anyway, stumbling his way through town, past the averted eyes of others, all the way to Siloam and a miracle bigger than he can possibly imagine. For the man is about to gain more than his eyesight alone. His newfound vision will turn the tables of his entire life. Before, he was defined by what he needed, but henceforth, he will be defined by what he gives.

Giving from Our Nothing

In one of His last post-resurrection encounters, recorded in John 21, Jesus is planning a campfire breakfast for his disciples on the shore of the Sea of Tiberias. He has everything He needs except the fish the disciples had set out to catch the night before.

But they've caught nothing. All night long and not a single fish. The men are tired and discouraged, and they have no idea that Jesus is waiting for them.

In the morning they see someone on the shore who looks strangely familiar. The man calls out over the water, "Cast the net on the right-hand side of the boat and you will find a catch." They squint. The command and the man who gives it seem eerily familiar. Another man, in a similar situation, offered the same direction three years ago. So they toss their nets into the water, and the boat is almost capsized by the catch. Astonished, the men set to hauling the fish into the boat. A few of them look toward the shore and wonder. John is the first to say it: "It is the Lord."

Peter jumps over the side of the boat and swims to Jesus. The rest of the fishermen pull hard on the oars. Soon they are onshore, laughing with Jesus and filling themselves with freshly grilled fish.

When they are finished with their breakfast and encouraged by their time with Jesus, the Lord asks Peter a question: "Simon, son of John, do you love Me more than these?" Peter—the same Peter who only days ago had betrayed Him three times—quickly affirms his love for Him. Jesus replies, "Tend My lambs."

He repeats His question two more times until Peter feels grieved. "Lord, You know all things," he says. "You know that I love You." In response, Jesus plants His last seed in Peter's soul before He ascends to His Father. It's an exclamation point in their relationship: "Tend My sheep."

At the tipping point of our own relationship with Jesus, He will ask us to do the same: "Tend My sheep." They are *His* sheep, but He chooses to look after them through a body of believers who have wounds that hamper them, character defects that disqualify them, fears that imprison them, and temperaments that sabotage them.

That's us. We are extensions of the Body that first gathered itself on the shore of the Sea of Tiberias.

Those of us who will offer our skin in the game can only give what we have to give. And so what if we have nothing of high value to give, except what we've been given by the Giver? The fish the disciples bring to the campfire breakfast are substantial, and all of them caught because of a word from the Master. We're all tempted to compare the value of what we have to give with the perceived value of what others give, because we believe that the basis of our risk is our own resources, not His. In one way or another, our gifts always seem overshadowed by another's.

One year, my old neighbor John decided to terrace his steep-sloping backyard—on his own. He drew up the plans, submitted them to the homeowners association, and used some kind of tri-pod-like thing to mark boundaries and levels. Then he shoveled away a mountain of rock, installed a new drainage system, cut and rolled all his sod, moved his sprinkler system, uprooted and replanted a tree, leveled his yard with a Bobcat, built all the forms for pouring a concrete patio and retaining walls, attached stone facades to the walls, and finally, re-sodded.

I watched all of John's activities wide-eyed and astonished. Whenever I checked on his progress, I found myself asking, "You're going to do *what?*" I felt so . . . pre-functional. So dwarfed by John's capabilities. I couldn't even keep our trees from dying of thirst, and here this guy across the street was engineering the Taj Mahal of landscaping projects. Inevitably, I compared my abilities with his. And inevitably, I was forced to agree with the one lie men tell themselves more than any other: I don't have what it takes.

If I believe the prerequisite to giving what I have to give is my own stockpiled treasure, my way forward is a hopeless path.

This is why no one but Jesus recognizes the remarkable act of giving by the widow who offers her "mite" to the public coffer—she has almost nothing to offer, but she offers what she has (Mark

12:41–44). In Jesus' eyes, she has given a fortune. And in pointing it out to His disciples, He's trying to say that the size of our contribution is irrelevant, as long as whatever we offer is whatever we have to give. He does not think the way we think—He simply wants our *everything*, no matter how inconsequential it might seem to us.

Just before His well-known miracle with the loaves and the fish, Jesus climbs the mountain with His disciples to sit and watch the crowds stream up the hill. Then He has an idea. With what I imagine is a glint in His eye, He turns to Philip and asks, "Where are we to buy bread, so that these may eat?" John tells us what was going on in Jesus' mind at that moment: "This he was saying to test him, for He Himself knew what He was intending to do."

Philip, shocked and even a little confused by Jesus' question, responds that it would take nothing less than a fortune to feed such a large crowd. And here's where an eavesdropping Andrew does something remarkable. Instead of simply scoffing at what Jesus has asked, he entertains the possibility that Jesus might be able to do a lot with a little. So he offers an idea that is neither rational nor practical. "There is a lad here who has five barley loaves and two fish," Andrew says, "but what are these for so many people?" In other words, the disciples have nearly no resources—but they do have *something*. And as we know from the rest of the story, that something proves to be more than enough in Jesus' hands.

In the same manner, Jesus wants us to give Him our own "something," no matter how insignificant or even laughable it seems. His question to us is, "Will you give everything you've got, even though you have nothing without Me?"

Let's return to Jesus' after-breakfast conversation with Peter by the Sea of Tiberias. Jesus is taking Peter back to the painful center of his greatest failure. Three times during Jesus' darkest hour, Peter had denied any association with Him. Now it appears that Jesus doubts Peter's love for Him. His questioning of Peter tears the scab off of a fresh wound.

Peter's Achilles' heel has always been his brash belief in himself. He attempts great things because he trusts in the "warhorse" of his personal resources (Ps. 33:16–17 NLT). So in this short interchange, Jesus is doing two things. He is subtly reminding Peter that the disciple's resources are bankrupt. Yet, in the face of that bankruptcy, He is also challenging Peter to give like he's never given before. Extrapolated, it comes across like this: *All you've ever really had is a "mustard seed" to give, Peter. But that's more than enough for Me to work with—so give it, and let Me take what is smaller than all other seeds and grow it into something that is "larger than the garden plants and becomes a tree, so that the birds of the air come and nest in its branches"* (Matt. 13:32).

When we face the bitter reality of our own insolvency and stop pretending we're bigger and better than we really are, then we are freed to give our everything without worrying about whether it's enough. Jesus makes it enough.

Big Knife, Little Girl

The other day, my ten-year-old daughter Emma told us she wanted to make dinner for all of us, and she wanted *absolutely* no help. She wanted the satisfaction of preparing everything herself from start to finish. My wife felt excited about the prospect. But my gut got tight—mostly because Emma wanted to have watermelon as our fruit for the evening, and she wanted to use our immense, horror-movie-like butcher knife to cut said watermelon. I said absolutely not. Bev said let her try, with a little help. Bev won.

In the process, Emma found out for herself that she needed a little help with that surgical procedure. But she did the job. We had a great dinner, and she got to feel the satisfaction of serving our whole family. As for me, I was reminded once again how very controlling I am when something—or someone—important to me is on the line.

Can you relate? If so, then we both admit that we're locked into a permanent wrestling match between control and trust.

Jesus does not wrestle in this way, though. He's already decided to trust us. He could do things on His own, give good gifts directly, but instead, He chooses to move through often-undependable people like us. Risk is the currency He requires of us in that partnership—some skin in the game on our part. We offer that currency, and He says, "That's all I need."

In Jesus' parables of the kingdom of God, He often used agricultural metaphors. The growing process that is common to all plants helps us understand what to expect as we lean forcefully into risk. The thirteenth chapter of Matthew is packed with sowing, growing, and reaping—and any farmer can tell you that the most basic risk in this process is the sowing of the seed. Skin in the game translates into a risky investment in the unseen and a determined expectation that time will turn the "seed" we plant into something big.

If waiting is intolerable to you, then you will develop a belief that sowing risk never produces a crop. Because those who risk well, wait well.

"And now, Lord, for what do I wait? My hope is in You" (Ps. 39:7).

FOR DISCUSSION OR PERSONAL REFLECTION

- What are some of the biggest risks you've taken in your life? How has your life been impacted—for good or bad—because of those risks?
- What are some impediments to risk in your life—that is, lies you have treated as truths?
- To whom in your life are you most likely to compare yourself right now, and why?

- When have you experienced God's taking a small thing you've offered Him and turning it into something big?
- Why would Jesus emphasize that in God's kingdom, things that seem tiny and insignificant can become huge and surpassingly significant when we offer them to Him?

CHAPTER 7

WILL YOU WAIT, EVEN WHEN ALL HOPE IS LOST?

The Story of Mary, Martha, and Their Dead Brother

"Waiting is painful. Forgetting is painful. But not knowing which to do is the worst kind of suffering."
—Paulo Coelho

Lazarus of Bethany is sick. Since he is not only the brother of Mary and Martha but also one of Jesus' best friends, the sisters send urgent word to Jesus that their brother needs Him . . . *now*.

And then Jesus does something incomprehensible to us at first blush. Because He "loved Martha and her sister and Lazarus," *He decides to wait two days before setting out to Bethany.*

The last time Jesus was in the region, He barely escaped an angry mob's plot to stone Him to death. But it is not because He's afraid to go back to Judea that He delays His trip. He waits because He *loves* the sisters and their brother. Jesus defends His confusing decision by telling His disciples that the sickness Lazarus has won't end in death, and that his delay represents an important opportunity for "the Son of God" to "be glorified by it."

But when Jesus finally shows up, his beloved friend has already been dead and buried for four days. Jesus' waiting has cost Lazarus his life and Mary and Martha wave upon wave of grief. What sort of "love" is that?

When Martha and Mary hear that Jesus is nearby, only Martha rushes to meet Him. Mary is too grief-stricken and, likely, furious at Jesus for waiting too long to help her brother.

Martha is blunt: "Lord, if You had been here, my brother would not have died." But then she puts her skin in the game, moving toward hope when there is no hope: "Even now I know that whatever You ask of God, God will give You." And Jesus, ever-bold, responds, "Your brother will rise again."

This sounds too good to be true, and Martha must make sure that she's not misinterpreting what "rise again" means. She says, "I know that he will rise again in the resurrection on the last day." But Jesus replies, "I am the resurrection and the life; he who believes in Me will live even if he dies, and everyone who lives and believes in Me will never die" (John 11:21–26).

The resurrection isn't a time or an event; it's a person. When we invite Jesus into the dark places in our life we're inviting resurrection into those places. And then comes His invitation to go all-in with Him: "Do you believe this?" That's the question He asks Martha. Will she trust in the Resurrection incarnate, who is standing in front of her?

And Martha, in response, shoves all her chips into the middle of the table. "Yes, Lord," she says, "I have believed that You are the Christ, the Son of God" (v. 27).

Waiting on God can kill our hope when the object of our waiting seems hopeless. Hoping when there is no hope does not guarantee the outcome, but the act of it does force to the surface a kind of abandon—a desperate plea for help that leaves us vulnerable to deep disappointment and grief. When we believe in the face of a hopeless cause, we are carving out a capacity in our soul to live by faith, not by sight. And faith is central to a skin-in-the-game life—one in which bold, risky giving of ourselves unlocks our ability to embrace each moment as a "living sacrifice."

We cannot learn to hope this way without learning how to wait.

Jesus asks Martha to tell her sister that He wants to see her, and Mary rushes to meet Him. She is weeping. And now He is weeping too. He asks to be led to the tomb and then orders the stone to be moved from the entrance. Martha warns Him of the stench that will be released, but Jesus reminds her, "Did I not say to you that if you believe, you will see the glory of God?" And they do. The dead man walks. But more than that, the Son of God is glorified—yes, this is a miracle that will end up shaking the ancient world, but it would not have happened had He not been willing to plunge His close friends into the crucible of waiting.

The Waiting Game

There are few things we hate more than waiting. That's ironic, because we do so much of it. Americans alone spend more than thirty-seven billion hours waiting in line every year. Why is the Department of Motor Vehicles so universally despised? Because we're in for a mind-numbing wait. What do we dread most about theme parks? The slow-moving, serpentine lines. What will make us stay home when we hoped to eat out? A long waiting list.

When Timex asked people how long they would wait before taking action in a wide variety of situations, researchers discovered that we'll consent to wait only

- thirteen seconds before we honk at a car in front of us that's stopped at a green light;

- twenty-six seconds before we shush people who are talking in a movie theater;
- twenty-six seconds before we take the seat of someone who's walked away;
- forty-five seconds before we ask someone who's talking too loud on a cell phone to "keep it down";
- thirteen minutes for a table at a restaurant;
- twenty minutes for a blind date to show up before we leave; and
- twenty minutes for the last person to show up for Thanksgiving dinner before we dig in.[1]

In a *New York Times* article, journalist Alex Stone tells the story of how executives at a Houston airport faced and then solved a cascade of passenger complaints about long waits at the baggage claim.[2] They first decided to hire more baggage handlers, reducing wait times to an industry-beating average of eight minutes. But complaints persisted. This made no sense to the executives until they discovered that, on the average, passengers took just one minute to walk to baggage claim, resulting in a hurry-up-and-wait situation. The walk time was not a problem; the remaining seven empty minutes of staring at the baggage carousel was. So, in a burst of innovation, the executives moved the arrival gates farther away from the baggage claim area. Passengers now had to walk much farther, but their bags were often waiting for them when they arrived. Problem solved. The complaints dropped.

Stone interviewed MIT operations researcher Richard Larson, the world's leading expert on waiting in lines (a heroic occupation, for sure), to discover the psychological underpinnings of our relationship with waiting. What happened at the Houston airport makes for a perfect illustration. According to Larson, the length of our wait is not as important as what we're doing while we wait. "Often the psychology of queuing is more important than the statistics of the wait itself," says Larson.[3] Essentially, we tolerate "occupied time" (for example, walking to baggage claim) far better than "unoccupied time" (such as standing at the baggage carousel). Give us something to do while we wait, and the wait becomes endurable.

This is why, so often, waiting on God feels like unoccupied time to us. We wait, but what is really happening behind the scenes of our life? Is God actually doing anything, or does He appear—as Jesus did when He delayed His journey to Bethany—to be unconcerned about what's on the line for us while we're waiting for Him? Waiting without any certainty of a payback on our waiting-time violates our fundamental sense of fairness.

Stone observes:

> Perhaps the biggest influence on our feelings about lines . . . has to do with our perception of fairness. The universally acknowledged standard is first come first served: any deviation is, to most, a mark of iniquity and can lead to violent queue rage. [For example], a man was stabbed at a Maryland post office by a fellow customer who mistakenly thought he'd cut in line. Professor Larson calls these unwelcome intrusions "slips" and "skips." . . . Fairness also dictates that the length of a line should be commensurate with the value of the product or service for which we're waiting. The more valuable it is, the longer one is willing to wait for it. Hence the supermarket express line, a rare, socially-sanctioned violation of first come first served, based on the assumption that no reasonable person thinks a child buying a candy bar should wait behind an old man stocking up on provisions for the Mayan apocalypse.[4]

We're willing to endure almost anything as long as we perceive that we're being treated fairly. This is what fuels Mary's rage when Jesus finally shows up: "When Mary came where Jesus was, she saw Him, and fell at His feet, saying to Him, 'Lord, if You had been here, my brother would not have died'" (John 11:32). Spent with grief and consumed by confusion and anger, Mary collapses in front of Jesus and spits out her case against Him. She, like Job centuries before her, acknowledges the authority of God to choose whether or not He'll show up, but she's infuriated by the unfairness of it. In such moments, God's character is in the dock, and we demand explanations.

So, again, why would Jesus *cause* all of this grief and anger by delaying His journey? Professor Larson tells us that if the outcome of our waiting is truly valuable, we do not feel cheated by the expense. But here, Lazarus has died and has been buried for four days. The unbelievably high cost of this unoccupied time is too much to bear if it does not lead to Lazarus's rescue. A future resurrection of the dead is no comfort to either sister.

Jesus shows up late to reorient the focus of our waiting. The one thing that will transform unoccupied time to occupied time is a kind of settling into His intimate presence.

Our faith—which is intimately linked to our determination to wait on Him—is in the person of Jesus, not the performance of Jesus. He's after a restoration of the kind of relationship He had with Adam and Eve before the first man and woman decided that God Himself was not enough for them. They wanted more, and that led to betrayal and brokenness and sin and shame. If that intimacy is to be restored, it will have to be fueled by the miracle of our choice to love God no matter what His performance, no matter how unoccupied our waiting seems to be.

John Ortberg writes, "Biblically, waiting is not just something we have to do until we get what we want. Waiting is part of the process of becoming what God wants us to be."[5]

Waiting on God is not about leveraging the outcome (though Jesus does not discourage us from asking—He did tell us that we "do not have because we do not ask"); it's about leveraging His presence. When Martha acknowledges that her brother will find life in a future resurrection, Jesus tells her that Life is already present and is close enough to touch. And as Mary sobs at His feet, her tears, rather than her anger, are leading her (and us) back to Jesus.

When I am locked in my own waiting room, hoping God will come through for me but feeling frightened and angered by His delay, I feel like an overwhelmed toddler. Like a cat threatened by a junkyard mongrel, I try to make myself appear as big as possible as a warning to my fears that they'd better stay away from me. But my tears always betray me; they strip away my facade and remind me that, at my core, my true self is always longing for restoration in my relationship with God.

My tears often drag me down my basement stairs, where a musty-smelling, paisley-orange couch with no feet sits flush against a concrete wall under a small garden-level window. There on that smelly old couch, I let the tears come. And I feel cleansed and *congruent* again, because I'm acknowledging my desperate thirst for the person of Jesus. Our tears in the midst of our waiting—which represent a vulnerable invitation for God to enter into our raw reality—transform unoccupied time into occupied time, leading us back into right relationship with Jesus.

Entering the Holy of Holies

N. T. Wright, the great contemporary British apologist, offers an unconventional explanation for why Jesus goes ballistic in Jerusalem's temple, heaving over the tables of the moneychangers and whipping them into a panicked exit. Yes, He is infuriated by the shysters who've turned this place of holy connection between God and His people into a first-century version of QVC. But He is also proclaiming, says Wright, "that this town isn't big enough for two Temples."[6]

The Jerusalem temple's purpose has always been to offer an outpost oasis of God's presence in the desert of humanity. But now *Jesus* is that outpost. In the incarnation, Jesus has supplanted the temple. And soon His Spirit will make His home inside the hearts of His followers. In the words of Paul the apostle, "Do you not know that you are a temple of God and that the Spirit of God dwells in you?" (1 Cor. 3:16). We enter into the Holy of Holies when we enter into Jesus. He in us, we in Him.

Jesus treats Mary's tears as an invitation to enter into her grief; He is "deeply moved in spirit and . . . troubled" (John 11:33). He asks where Lazarus has been laid to rest, and when they show Him, He begins to weep.

Deeply moved. Troubled. Weeping. This is how Jesus responds to Mary's tears and how He will respond to ours. It is an intimate, shared exchange that replaces the currency of performance with the currency of connection. It is our raw intimacy with Jesus, kindled by what happens in the waiting rooms of our life, that transforms "unoccupied" to "occupied." Somewhere in the crucible of our waiting, we find ourselves occupied by Jesus Himself. Though we despise the leverage, we prize the Person we are leveraged toward. And when we draw near to Jesus in this way, His presence—or more accurately, His *essence*—will consume us.

In *Waiting On God*, Simone Weil writes,

The beauty of the world is the mouth of a labyrinth. The unwary individual who on entering takes a few steps is soon unable to find the opening. Worn out, with nothing to eat or drink, in the dark, separated from his dear ones, and from everything he loves and is accustomed to, he walks on without knowing anything or hoping anything, incapable even of discovering whether he is really going forward or merely turning round on the same spot. But this affliction is as nothing compared with the danger threatening him. For if he does not lose courage, if he goes on walking, it is absolutely certain that he will finally arrive at the center of the labyrinth. And there God is waiting to eat him. Later he will go out again, but he will be changed, he will have become different, after being eaten and digested by God. Afterward he will stay near the entrance so that he can gently push all those who come near into the opening.[7]

Jesus, for His part, is always moving us from a transactional relationship with Him ("If You give me what I want, I will give You what You want") to something that looks and feels more like two lovers who can't take their eyes off one another. This is what happens in both Martha and Mary, each in her own way. Their interactions with Jesus in the context of His delay move from a transaction (both of them cry out, "Lord, if You had been here, my brother would not have died") to something that's much closer to Weil's "eaten and digested" (Martha's declaration, "Yes, Lord; I have believed that You are the Christ, the Son of God," and Mary's tears of pain, vulnerability, and invitation).

The same was true for Job, locked inside one of the worst waiting rooms in history. Nearing the end of his travail, he moved from unoccupied time ("Why doesn't the Almighty bring the wicked to judgment? Why must the godly wait for him in vain?" [Job 24:1 NLT]) to the intimacy of occupied time ("I had only heard about you before, but now I have seen you with my own eyes. I take back everything I said, and I sit in dust and ashes to show my repentance" [Job 42:5-6 NLT]).

Not long ago, a friend invited me to help him lead a men's retreat. In preparation, he wanted to show me an intense scene from the Christian film *Facing the Giants*, because he was planning to use it as an "orbital center" for the retreat. I hadn't seen the film because, frankly, I doubted that I'd like it. But the scene my friend showed me, depicting the innovative way a coach found to prod a slacker football player to greatness, *did* move me.

My friend then showed me the discussion questions he planned to use, focusing on the courage it takes to give everything you have. I told him there's a hidden trap in that trajectory, because many think that the answer to everything is trying harder.

That includes being patient when we're stuck in our waiting rooms. Simply working harder at being patient isn't the answer. It is, of course, important to persevere, but what happens when you reach the end of your ability to try hard? At that desolate place—the same place Martha and Mary and you and I have sometimes wallowed—we can give up on trying hard and give everything to Him. In "losing our life" to Him we somehow gain the courage we need to offer our skin in the game. When we "lose our life" to Him, that's when we find it.

The kind of waiting that is risky and courageous isn't about trying harder; it's about the stamina produced by a closer "orbit" around Jesus.

Stamina, Not Data or Technique

According to researchers at the Institute of Cognitive Sciences and Technologies (ICST), "The ability to delay gratification is a turning point in the development of any child and a hallmark of advanced cognition in many species. Nevertheless, most animals cannot withstand delays longer than few seconds, even when substantial rewards are at stake, and also humans are often strongly averse to waiting."[8]

Um, "strongly averse" might be an understatement. But ICST scientists have discovered in their research a fascinating connection between the ability to *wait* and the ability to *magnify our impact*. It turns out that species that exhibit "remarkable tolerance for delay" also have "uncanny ability in tool use" (capuchin monkeys, for example).

Why is this relevant to us? Because Jesus came to set captives free—that's at the core of His mission. And He has invited us into

His mission. We are always closer to living out of our true identity when we are involved with Jesus in setting captives free. But this sort of adventure requires the ability to bring magnified impact into others' lives. And waiting in hope is one of the things that empowers this impact. By driving us into an occupied time of intimacy with Jesus, it produces in us a stamina that can change people, relational systems, and, ultimately, the world.

In *A Failure of Nerve*, author, business consultant, therapist, rabbi, and family systems expert Edwin Friedman explains how stamina, not using strategy or technique or data to try harder, is the true engine driving good impact in others' lives:

> Conceptually stuck systems cannot become unstuck simply by trying harder. For a fundamental reorientation to occur, that spirit of adventure which optimizes serendipity and which enables new perceptions beyond the control of our thinking processes must happen first. This is equally true regarding families, institutions, whole nations, and entire civilizations. . . . But for that type of change to occur, the system in turn must produce leaders who can both take the first step and maintain the stamina to follow through in the face of predictable resistance and sabotage. Any renaissance, anywhere, whether in a marriage or a business, depends primarily not only on new data and techniques, but on the capacity of leaders to separate themselves from the surrounding emotional climate so that they can break through the barriers that are keeping everyone from "going the other way."[9]

Friedman could be describing the "stamina" Jesus displays when he waits to go to Bethany, even though his close friend lies dying. He knows that our collective sin has created a "stuck system" that excludes us from the Holy of Holies of His intimate presence, and that a "fundamental reorientation" is therefore required. The template of that transformation in our relationship with Him is played out with Martha and Mary. Friedman's description of stamina follows exactly the strange and unpredictable behavior of Jesus in His encounter with these two close friends.

To adopt Friedman's language, Jesus takes the first step and maintains the stamina to follow through in the face of predictable resistance. In the process, he separates Himself from the surrounding emotional climate so He can break through the barriers that are keeping everyone from "going the other way." And here, "going the other way" means turning back to enter the Holy of Holies—the very heart of Jesus. There, in that place of intimacy, He consummates our relationship by sharing everything He has with us, including the stamina we need to participate in His mission to set captives free.

Jesus forces us into the waiting room because He loves us, just as He loved Martha and Mary and Lazarus. But, as G. K. Chesterton says, "If you meet the Jesus of the gospels, you must redefine what love is, or you won't be able to stand him."

FOR DISCUSSION OR PERSONAL REFLECTION

- How do you handle waiting? Are you usually a "good wait-er" or a "bad wait-er"?
- What "redeems" the times in your life when you have to wait for something or someone?
- When was there a season of your life that was characterized by waiting on God? What happened in you as a result of the waiting?
- Sometimes in our seasons of waiting on God, we don't see the thing we hoped for. Do seasons with such an outcome draw you to God or repel you from Him? Explain.

- How has this John Ortberg quote been true in your life? "Biblically, waiting is not just something we have to do until we get what we want. Waiting is part of the process of becoming what God wants us to be."[10]
- Do you typically welcome or resist tears? When you do allow yourself to cry, what impact does that have on you?
- What does this quote from Simone Weil mean to you? "For if he does not lose courage, if he goes on walking, it is absolutely certain that he will finally arrive at the center of the labyrinth. And there God is waiting to eat him."[11]
- If a friend asked you to explain the following G. K. Chesterton quote, what would you say? "If you meet the Jesus of the gospels, you must redefine what love is, or you won't be able to stand him."[12]

CHAPTER 8

WILL YOU MAKE JESUS YOUR FIRST AND LAST RESORT?

The Story of Peter, Tied to the Mast

"First she said we were to keep clear of the Sirens, who sit and sing most beautifully in a field of flowers; but she said I might hear them myself so long as no one else did. Therefore, take me and bind me to the crosspiece half way up the mast; bind me as I stand upright, with a bond so fast that I cannot possibly break away, and lash the rope's ends to the mast itself. If I beg and pray you to set me free, then bind me more tightly still."
—Odysseus, from Homer's Odyssey, Book XII

At the height of His popularity, when Jesus has gathered the kind of fervent mass support that all rebels and revolutionaries must have to overthrow their oppressors, He does something that is guaranteed to open wide the drain on His burgeoning influence.

First, He tells the crowds that He is not another flash-in-the-pan prophet—He has come down out of heaven. This doesn't sit well with those who were ready to follow Him as a king-in-waiting; they are not ready to align with a man who thinks He's God. Then Jesus ups the ante with this: "I am the living bread that came down out of heaven; if anyone eats of this bread, he will live forever; and the bread also which I will give for the life of the world is My flesh" (John 6:51). Similar to our own response had we been there, Jesus' followers are now positively disillusioned with their rock-star rabbi: "How can this man give us *His* flesh to eat?" "Cannibalism," the crowd murmurs.

Jesus has a chance to clear up this misunderstanding—to quickly recover Himself, as any skilled politician would do. But instead He pours fuel on the fire: "Truly, truly, I say to you, unless you eat the flesh of the Son of Man and drink His blood, you have no life in yourselves. He who eats My flesh and drinks My blood has eternal life. . . . For My flesh is true food, and My blood is true drink. He who eats My flesh and drinks My blood abides in Me, and I in him" (vv. 53–56).

The backlash to Jesus' inscrutable repetition of "Eat My body and drink My blood" is easy to predict. The masses who venerate Him for His miracles and His teaching now turn on Him because He clearly must be insane. Closer to home, many of His own disciples feel forced to quit Him—they just don't know how to process the destruction of their expectations. They have followed Jesus because He had promise as a revolutionary, the Messiah who would bring Israel freedom from its oppressors and restoration as a sovereign nation.

There is method behind Jesus' madness—He is winnowing those who've pledged allegiance to Him by asking them to wholly ingest Him. This is no wine-tasting party He's inviting them to, where they can swill a little Jesus around in their mouth and then spit Him out, so to speak. The invitation is to a feast. But His disciples are just as disillusioned as the masses. "This is a difficult statement; who can listen to it?" they say. On this day many will stop following Him because of His insistence that He is God. In response, Jesus asks those who remain a question that would seem desperate if you or I had asked it: "You do not want to go away also, do you?"

But Jesus is not asking because He is insecure—He's asking because it is time to discover who has skin in the game. When the crowd turns and the benefits of following Jesus are significantly outweighed by the risks, only those who are willing to identify with Jesus will stay. And Peter steps into this moment and owns it: "Lord, to whom shall we go? You have words of eternal life. We have believed and have come to know that You are the Holy One of God" (vv. 67–68).

In Homer's great epic, *The Odyssey*, the hero, Ulysses, is tied to the mast of his ship so he can withstand the deadly allure of the sirens' singing.[1] He is committed; no matter what happens to him, he will stay with his ship.

Like Ulysses, Peter is lashing himself to the mast, which is Jesus. He may not understand everything that Jesus says, but he understands something much more important—the heart of Jesus. And that's all Peter needs to know. "To whom shall we go?" is the DNA of skin in the game. Peter is saying, in essence, "I will go down with this ship, tied to the mast."

Jesus brings the twelve to this moment because He will not continue in His redemptive mission with followers who have not tied themselves to His mast. He has brought them to the brink of a skin-in-the-game choice: *Will you make Me the main course of your life, or will you treat Me like the flavor of the day?* It is the same choice we must make if we intend to accept Jesus' invitation to share in His mission.

It's not a choice we like, though. We'd prefer to treat Jesus as if He were just an enhancement to our lives. Post-resurrection Peter and his mates would scoff at this notion. Jesus asked his followers to die for Him. He wanted it all.

Look at the disturbing story of Ananias and Sapphira (Acts 5:1–15

NIV). Because they lied about how much "skin in the game" they'd actually invested, they paid with their lives. The result? "Great fear seized the whole church" and "no one else dared join [the apostles]." Well, of course. A lot of people who wanted to fit Jesus into their lives were repelled when they learned the price for following him was . . . everything.

Shark, Not Dolphin

In the iconic first season of *Saturday Night Live*, the legendary sketch comedians spoofed the recent release of the 1975 movie *Jaws* by introducing a recurring character called the Land Shark. The skits featured a guy dressed in a shark outfit, voiced by Chevy Chase. The Land Shark stalked his prey by knocking on apartment doors and pretending to be a repairman, a door-to-door salesman, or a deliveryman. Once the victim opened the door, the Land Shark would rush in and swallow his prey.

> *[Scene: A New York apartment. Someone knocks on the door.]*
> WOMAN, *not opening the door.* Yes?
> VOICE, *MUMBLING.* Mrs. Arlsburgerhhh?
> WOMAN. What?
> VOICE, *MUMBLING.* Mrs. Johannesburrrr?
> WOMAN. Who is it?
> VOICE. *(Pause.)* Flowers.
> WOMAN. Flowers for whom?
> VOICE. *(Long pause.)* Plumber, ma'am.
> WOMAN. I don't need a plumber. You're that clever shark,
>   aren't you?
> VOICE. *(Pause.)* Candygram.
> WOMAN. Candygram, my foot. You get out of here before
>   I call the police. You're the shark, and you know it.
> VOICE: Wait. I . . . I'm only a dolphin, ma'am.

WOMAN: A dolphin? Well . . . okay. *(Opens door.)*
[*Huge latex and foam-rubber shark head lunges through open
    door, chomps down on woman's head, and drags her out of
    the apartment, all while the* Jaws *attack music is playing.*][2]

Buried in the Land Shark skit is a near-perfect parable for why
so many of us have kept Jesus at a distance in our lives. A life that's
consumed by love for Him isn't a *functional reality* for many of us
because we've really, at our core, prepared ourselves for a dolphin,
not a shark. We've cobbled together a mix-and-match, nice-guy Jesus
using bits and pieces of the things He said and did. Unconsciously,
we reassure ourselves that the Shark on the other side of our soul's
door (which is the Jesus described in the Bible) is really a dolphin—
that is, a friendly, benign mystic who, like a trained porpoise, exists
to entertain our desires and delight our sensibilities. That's who
we'll open the door to. We won't open the door if we think there's a
shark on the other side.

Because, of course, if He's really a shark, then He might just eat
us alive.

It's fine to learn from Jonah's harrowing experience in the belly
of the fish, but we don't want to *be* Jonah. And yet, Jesus wants a
consuming relationship with us—an unrestrained giving of ourselves
to Him and He to us. Complete intimacy, in other words; the kind
of two-become-one intimacy that characterizes marriage. Quoting
the Old Testament, Jesus said, "'For this reason a man will leave
his father and mother and be united to his wife, and the two will
become one flesh.' So they are no longer two, but one" (Matt. 19:5–6
NIV). *Two but one* is *consuming* talk.

C. S. Lewis skewered the whole idea of a harmless, tamable Jesus
in the first of his Narnia books, *The Lion, the Witch and the Wardrobe.*
Lewis used a different metaphor than a shark, but the message is
the same. After the Pevensie children stumble through a door in the
back of a magical wardrobe into a fantastic alternate world ruled

by an evil witch and populated with talking animals, they're taken in by the Beavers, a husband and wife who've joined the insurgency against the witch. The Beavers tell the children about Aslan, the great lion king who has promised to return and lead them in defeating the witch. The Beavers are sure that the arrival of the children signals the return of Aslan and the final release from their cursed and frozen existence. But to the children's sensibilities, Aslan sounds frightening, mysterious, and vaguely threatening.

> "Is—is he a man?" asked Lucy.
>
> "Aslan a man!" said Mr. Beaver sternly. "Certainly not. I tell you he is the King of the wood and the son of the great Emperor-beyond-the-Sea. Don't you know who is the King of Beasts? Aslan is a lion—*the* Lion, the great Lion."
>
> "Ooh!" said Susan, "I'd thought he was a man. Is he—quite safe? I shall feel rather nervous about meeting a lion."
>
> "That you will, dearie, and no mistake," said Mrs. Beaver, "if there's anyone who can appear before Aslan without their knees knocking, they're either braver than most or else just silly."
>
> "Then he isn't safe?" said Lucy.
>
> "Safe?" said Mr. Beaver. "Don't you hear what Mrs. Beaver tells you? Who said anything about safe? 'Course he isn't safe. But he's good. He's the King, I tell you."[3]

Unsafe but good. We've heard this one before. And something in our soul knows it's true; the older we get, the more we have experienced how unsafe it is to follow Jesus. Amid the disappointment of our unmet hopes and dreams and the agony of our wounds and struggles, Jesus remains frustratingly good. He does not always do what we *want*, but is always doing what we *need*—and His estimation of the difference between these two words sometimes rankles us.

Like the Pevensie children, we naturally recoil from "unsafe."

Aslan is unpredictable and fierce—two words that also describe the biblical Jesus and, if we've laid ourselves bare to Him, our personal experience of Him in our life. That's the difference between a dolphin and a shark and a tame lion versus a wild one—*the* wild Lion. The biblical Jesus is at war with the Jesus we prefer—the edited Jesus, the partial Jesus, the flavor-of-the-day Jesus, the dolphin Jesus.

Some years ago I was invited, out of the blue, to serve on an advisory panel for the most ambitious study of Americans' faith beliefs and practices ever conducted. It was called the National Study of Youth and Religion, led by respected Notre Dame social researcher Dr. Christian Smith. The study was broader than its name implies because it included parents, not just teenagers. Chris and his research team conducted extensive phone interviews with more than three thousand young people, then interviewed one parent in each of their homes. After that, the team sampled from that huge pool and did half-day, face-to-face interviews with about three hundred teenagers to flesh out the answers to their phone interview questions. The team produced a rich vein of data, stories, and personal experiences, and from that, they created a first-of-its-kind, comprehensive sketch of what American kids and adults both believe, and how they live out those beliefs. The condensed outcome of what Chris's team discovered can be summed-up in one sentence:

Most American parents and teenagers describe a God who is like a divine butler or cosmic therapist.[4]

Jesus' job, according to this mind-set, is to help us do what we want, make us happy, and solve our problems.

Extrapolating further, Smith and his team described a nation of people whose religion, in practice, transcends established spiritual traditions and denominations. Smith's team labeled it "Moralistic, Therapeutic Deism" (MTD).

- *Moralistic* means our goal in life is to be a good person who conforms to the "rules of right conduct," as established by conventional wisdom.
- *Therapeutic* means that God exists for our pleasure, not the other way around. Faith in God is important because God can help us get what we want in life.
- *Deism* means that God is essentially unknowable—He exists, He's a moral lawgiver and judge, and He sometimes, unpredictably, gets involved in our lives. But we can't, and don't really want to, have an ongoing and intimate relationship with Him.[5]

Obviously, this isn't the gospel of Jesus Christ. Moralistic, Therapeutic Deism isn't even about Him. It's about making life work for us by conforming our idea of God into a custom-crafted *someone* who will meet our present needs, whatever they are. It's about getting what we want with as little skin in the game as we can get away with. There's no real expectation of a relationship with Jesus for followers of MTD, so intimacy is not even on the radar screen. Moreover, if MTD is really about making life work for us, then the functional way we relate to Jesus is performance-oriented: we think He exists to perform for us the way dolphins do at Sea World.

Our prayer lives bear this out. If we could record what we say to God, it would be obvious that our prayers are dominated by pleas and subtle demands for God to perform. Since we live in a fallen world, we're constantly in need of His help, rescue, and "blessings" just to navigate our personal mine fields. At least, that's how it seems. In the last few years, my own family's healthcare costs have rocketed from about $4,000 a year to more than $20,000. That body blow has affected my relationship with Jesus, moving it from "date night at a nice restaurant" to "business meeting at McDonalds." The gravitational pull of my pressing needs tempts me to relate to Jesus like he's a talisman—an impersonal power who can deliver for me.

The same mind-set also characterized the crowds that were magnetically drawn to a Jesus who spectacularly healed the sick, raised the dead, cast out demons, and produced massive amounts of food from thin air. He had fast become the flavor of the day for a famished and fickle crowd.

But didn't Jesus tell us, in John 14:14 (NIV), "You may ask me for anything in my name, and I will do it"? Yes, but Jesus made that promise in this context: "Very truly I tell you, whoever believes in me will do the works I have been doing, and they will do even greater things than these, because I am going to the Father." So "Ask me for anything" essentially means "If you give your life over to me and trust in who I am, I will fuel your deepest desires, because they are also My deepest desires." It has nothing to do with saying the right words so Jesus will jump through a flaming ring for us.

If we want a Jesus who will perform for us, our only practical choice is to ignore the biblical Jesus' shark-like nature and make believe we're dealing with a tame, trainable dolphin. Because if it's really a shark on the other side of the door, He might want all of us, not just some of us.

The Consuming Fire

Jesus attracted massive crowds because His actions and His teaching shocked and surprised people. He was the most successful performance artist of His time. Drawn by His supernatural fireworks, the crowds grew and grew. Thousands traveled far and sat in the dirt just to get a glimpse of Him. But the people let Him through their front doors because they were convinced He was nothing more than a "good teacher"—the title they habitually attached to Him. They of course understood that God is a "consuming fire" (Deut. 4:24), but it was ludicrous, blasphemous, and patently offensive to equate this carpenter's son from the backwater town of Nazareth with God.

Yet the consumption message is at the core of Jesus' teaching. It's not possible to have deeper intimacy with Him without eventually consuming Him and being consumed by Him. We may give Him permission to enter our heart because we believe He's a dolphin, but we're really opening our door to a shark.

Taped to my computer stand are two photos. I've looked at them thousands of times over the years. I put the first one there many years ago, when my coworkers and I each had to bring an old photo of ourselves to work for a team-building activity. I brought in one of myself when I was maybe three years old, and afterward I taped it where it is now, because I didn't want to forget that little guy. The photo is one of those "professional" shots with a fake background. I'm holding a ball just outside the frame, and I'm smiling. My hair is curly—curly and big. I'm impossibly freckled. And I'm wearing a sort of shirt-and-overall ensemble that you might describe as vaguely Scandinavian.

Often that photo is just part of the wallpaper of my cluttered office space. But sometimes I stop and look into that little boy's eyes, trying to find the "me" in there. And sometimes I find him. When I do, I feel compassion and affection for that little guy. Today I know what he's feeling, but he was clueless at the time. That shy little smile and slightly cautious look in his eyes means he feels sort of lost and alone and insignificant. He's sending out signals, hoping he'll get some bounce-back responses that offer clues to his identity. He's almost wholly dependent on the "mirrors" around him to reflect back to him whether there's any "there there."

Mostly, I know that, over time, that little guy came to believe there was an empty space where his soul was supposed to be—that there was no core at the core of his identity. And I know he was frightened by this, frightened that he'd be exposed and sent out of the community-of-people-with-real-souls like a leper during the time of Jesus.

So what's a little guy like him to do? Well, it makes perfect sense that he'd go looking around for an appropriate mask that would fool others into thinking he had a real face.

Just after college, I read a book by C. S. Lewis called *Till We Have Faces*. This was during a pseudo-intellectual phase of my life when I fashioned myself as the sort of guy who could understand *Till We Have Faces*. The truth is, there was a whole lot I didn't understand about that book—it's a retelling of an ancient Greek myth and a metaphor for maturing in Christ. Likely, the subconscious reason I attempted to read this book was the promise of its title: I knew I didn't have a real face, and I sure wanted one.

When you're wearing a mask that you hope people will mistake for your real face, you don't want people studying you. It's in your best interests to look away from people; to gravitate, metaphorically, toward dimly lit rooms; and to never, ever let someone peek behind the mask. The problem with wearing a mask all the time is that you're also continually trying your hardest to live up to it—to convince everyone, especially yourself, that the mask is the real you.

In my case, after I committed my life to Christ in fourth or fifth grade, I tried to use biblical principles and shallow archetypes of what I thought a Christian was supposed to be as my mask. And here's a surprise: I found that the church was set up to fuel this tips-and-techniques approach to life. In fact, if I had to condense the overarching message of most of the sermons I heard, it would be, "You can have a happier, nicer life if you'll just try harder in these 532 areas. Here are the principles you need to apply."

I bought into that message because it fit perfectly with my try-harder approach to life and my studied commitment to the masquerade. In fact, my high school friend Wally Wharton, in an act of prescience that's startling in retrospect, wrote this in my yearbook: "You're the hardest try-er I've ever known." I remember this now because of how weird it was: someone in high school actually said something to me that was more than halfway true. The other entries in my yearbook are screechy platitudes in comparison. And I remember his words now with sorrow, not the flush of pride I felt back then. The sorrow is there because Wally was right.

I wish I had asked myself, *"Why am I trying so hard?"*

The second picture taped to my computer stand is cut out from a magazine. An old friend gave it to me as a joke. It's one of that old TV sitcom character Gomer Pyle, the doofus Army private played by Jim Nabors. I guess I must have compared myself to Gomer Pyle once, and my friend happened to see a picture of him in a magazine, so he cut it out and gave it to me. I taped it right next to the picture of me as a three-year-old.

Maybe I resonated with Gomer Pyle because he discovered the key to life: When you subconsciously lower others' expectations, you find out it's not that hard to impress people. That's about the best a mask-wearing guy can hope for.

But the only way I could maintain my mask-wearing, tips-and-techniques Christian life was if Jesus behaved Himself. If He obeyed my demand to stay in his dolphin persona, I'd continue to invite Him in. I could not afford to be *consumed* by Him.

That is the blunt truth that got exposed after my wife asked me to leave and we were separated for three months. When I was invited to come back home, I returned with a sort of muted joy. I had deep apprehensions. The mask had been ripped off of my face, but I had no idea how to live life without it. The lie that had kept me in prison for more than thirty years had finally been revealed, and I had others around me urging (and counting on) me to live in freedom. But freedom meant that I had to offer myself to Jesus—to open myself to Him even though I now knew He was the consuming shark I'd feared, not the friendly dolphin I had always thought I needed.

It took me awhile to open my prison door to Jesus the shark, but I did. He means to consume me, but he won't attack me like Chevy Chase's Land Shark. Instead, He invites me to be consumed. I've been learning how to live as a free man ever since.

Freedom means the discovery of relational intimacy—with my wife, my friends, and certainly with God. Intimacy requires a face, not a mask, and I finally had a face. It wasn't a movie-star face or even a reality-show face, but at least it was mine. I didn't know at the time that my real face would eventually make it hard for me to feel comfortable, or even tolerant, around the masquerades that surrounded me. You come to hate the thing you were addicted to because it insinuates itself as a friend when it's actually a destroyer. And you come to despise the dolphin-like ways that you and so many others have wrongly attributed to Jesus.

I discovered that my mask had not only prevented others from seeing me but had also prevented me from seeing them. This was profoundly true about the way I'd seen Jesus. Incapable of true intimacy, I swam in shallow waters with Him. My friends would've disputed that description, because no one was more serious about his relationship with Jesus than me. But I've noticed that pretty much every married couple looks seriously in love at some point in the marriage, yet a lot of them get divorced. You can launch yourself toward intimacy, but that doesn't mean you're going to achieve orbit. And I certainly hadn't with Jesus. Now, without the mask, I often found myself startled, intrigued, and even whiplashed by the Jesus I could see full-faced.

The face I have today is the face Jesus has given me. In it, you can see that little freckle-faced boy and a little Gomer Pyle. But now there's a light somewhere behind there as well. Maybe it's the shine of God's glory; maybe it's the glint of shark teeth. It's the face God has always seen but I never did. It's the face God told me I have. It's the face He's promised is my very own, the result of a consuming relationship with Jesus—He in me and I in Him.

That's what happens when Jesus is the main course in our life, not just an appetizer. Feeding on Him and allowing ourselves to be consumed by Him frees us from the captivity of our masks, because we have given ourselves over to a Jesus who will not behave Himself.

My friend Ned Erickson describes his own path into a consuming relationship with Jesus this way:

Brennan Manning writes that the only way we can know anything for certain about God is by what we know about Jesus. Anything that is true about Jesus is true about God; anything untrue is untrue. It made sense. It might sound elementary to you. But it was life-changing for me. Besides, it was easy enough to try. So I started to get to know Jesus. I chose Mark. It's the shortest gospel, and I began reading real slow. I paid attention to everything the man said, did, and didn't do. And before I knew it, everything had changed. He became *real*. He knocked me head over heels. I wanted to know more—to know *Him more*—deeply, intimately. And slowly, like a ship coming out of the fog, I began to see Him, smell Him, feel Him. I knew what His voice sounded like. And it only made me want more.

At the same time, it was like He started rubbing off on me. I started noticing things I never noticed before—leaves changing color, the sound of water hitting the sink. My ears listened differently. To people. I began hearing the questions they were asking underneath the questions they were asking. I watched television with new eyes. My judgmental spirit was gone. I cried at odd moments. I found myself liking the sensation I got when I helped other people. It was crazy.

And the craziest part: It was like all of a sudden I had found myself. It was like the more I got to know Jesus, the more he introduced me to the person he created: Me. The real me. The one that, if I am honest, I have always been afraid of. Because what if I don't like the real me? Or what if the real me does something stupid? Or what if the real me really isn't that cool? Or what if the real me gets hurt? But for the first time, with Jesus' encouragement, I was willing to give me a try. I have never felt so much pain, been so broken, so weak, so pathetic, so vulnerable. It has been the hardest experience of my life. And it has been the best. Because now I know—now *I know*—that I am loved. Jesus loves me! Me! In all my mess, the way I am. Not only that, He likes me! If He had a free afternoon (and He does, countless ones), He would choose to spend it with me. And I would spend it with Him.[6]

Devoured into Life

Transformation, many will say, comes from trying harder in all of the shoulds of the gospel. But transformation actually comes from our getting closer to Jesus, much like radioactivity affects us the closer we get to its source.

Jesus' parable of the hidden treasure in Matthew 13 is a great example. Why did the man sell everything he had to buy the field? Because he had a thorough understanding and appreciation for the treasure he knew was buried there. It was apparently a treasure visible to many but not appreciated for its inestimable value. The "formula" is simple: If you understand the value and beauty of the treasure, you'll give up everything to get it. You don't have to convince or cajole anybody to pursue something that is both priceless and attainable.

But most people have not gone all-in for the treasure that is Jesus. Why not? Because they've been told of His surpassing value by others, but they haven't arrived at that assessment themselves.

Our purpose, as followers of Jesus, is to lift up the treasure—to examine it well and explain its rare and priceless facets—so that others can come to appreciate its value. Then no "shoulds" are necessary. Follow-through happens naturally once a person recognizes the treasure for what it is. Once that happens, it's not that big a deal to offer our skin in the game. A deeper taste of Jesus makes us want to risk our widow's mite, the only trifle we have, on Him.

In *Good to Great*, author Jim Collins and his team of researchers studied eleven companies that beat the odds and vaulted out of long-time mediocrity into longtime excellence. One transforming catalyst is something Collins calls the "Hedgehog Concept."[7] It means that companies that embrace one simple purpose and then pursue it with passion succeed. Conversely, companies that skittered from one purpose to another stayed mired in mediocrity.

Understanding the true value of the treasure in the field produces a single driving passion that motivates us, like Peter, to tie ourselves to the mast of Jesus.

So . . . here is what happens when you let the Land Shark in: He eats you alive—and then you're *alive*. You think you're a goner, and then you taste life for the first time. Like Jonah, we are swallowed by the "great fish," and then we enter what turns out not to be the belly of the beast but the Promised Land. The Promised Land is a place where it's impossible to see anything, hear anything, taste anything, smell anything, and experience anything that doesn't remind you of Jesus. He's not just camping out in your world, *He is your world.*

When you're consumed by Jesus, you experience the same transition that Dorothy experienced when her house flew out of Kansas and landed in Oz. Ned describes it this way:

> I think that becoming more like Jesus means I'm beginning to see things the way He sees things, the way things really are. Maybe it means I'm beginning to enjoy people the way He enjoys them, to hurt for people the way He hurts for them, to understand culture the way He does, to be aware of things. It's not about being taken over by Him. It's about being connected to Him in such a way that your ears listen the way His do, your eyes see the way His does, your heart, your mind. Becoming like Jesus really is the only way to see, hear, taste, smell, and touch. It makes it possible for us to emotionally relate with each other and spiritually understand reality—the way things really are.[8]

Jesus is no dolphin—and that is our salvation. Only a man-eater could win a face-off with the Evil One. The prize? My soul, your soul. Nothing in life compares to getting swallowed by Jesus, then finding that we've entered not into darkness but into the light of our true identity. It's the electrified life we experience when we finally realize we have a real face, and can wholeheartedly offer our skin in the game.

FOR DISCUSSION OR PERSONAL REFLECTION

- Would others who know you say that you've "tied yourself to the mast" of Jesus? Why or why not?
- In what ways have you preferred Jesus as a mere enhancement to your life rather than an all-or-nothing Jesus who requires you to "tie yourself to the mast"?
- What about the idea of Jesus as a shark rather than a dolphin repels you—or attracts you?
- In what ways do you observe people following the "functional religion" of Moralistic, Therapeutic Deism? How do you sometimes treat God as a divine butler or cosmic therapist?
- In your life, when have you felt consumed by God or that you are consuming Him? What does that look like for you?
- Have you generally experienced church as a tips-and-techniques place or as a place that draws you into deeper intimacy with Jesus? Explain.
- What masks do you wear, if any, that prevent people from seeing who you really are?
- Is it hard or easy for you to believe that if Jesus had a free afternoon, He'd choose to spend it with you? Explain.
- In what ways have you begun to see as Jesus sees, hear as He hears, smell as He smells, and touch as He touches?

EPILOGUE

Earl Palmer, the beloved and now-retired pastor of First Presbyterian Church in Berkeley, California, once countered critics who rail against the church for its hypocritical, scandalous, and often irrelevant footprint in the culture. "When the Milpitas High School orchestra attempts Beethoven's Ninth Symphony, the result is appalling," he said. "I wouldn't be surprised if the performance made old Ludwig roll over in his grave despite his deafness. You might ask: 'Why bother? Why inflict on those poor kids the terrible burden of trying to render what the immortal Beethoven had in mind? Not even the great Chicago Symphony Orchestra can attain that perfection.' My answer is this: The Milpitas High School orchestra will give some people in that audience their only encounter with Beethoven's great Ninth Symphony. Far from perfection, it is nevertheless the only way they will hear Beethoven's message."[1]

Palmer is pointing out that the only way a starving, thirsty, deluded, and suffering world will ever hear the music of the gospel is through the body of Christ, arguably the worst "high school orchestra" ever to disgrace a bandstand. If performance standards are really the most important measure, then the church is in trouble. But God is determined to trade the perfection of His solo performance for the possibility of playing a little improvisational jazz with us, the screechy saxophone players in the kingdom of God's ragtag big band.

Why?

The answer is obvious to anyone who understands Jesus' saying, "You must become like little children"—because children will sing, with unabashed glee, "Jesus loves me, this I know." Those three words, "Jesus loves me," are the cornerstone of mission in the kingdom of God. God has sacrificed everything—not only His Son but also His performance standards—to draw us back into intimate relationship with Himself. But He has not won us back so we can sit idly on the sidelines while we watch Him work. No, no, no.

He wants teammates, not fans.

God reminds us, "My thoughts are not your thoughts, nor are your ways My ways" (Isa. 55:8). That's maybe the most glaring understatement in the Bible. God could ensure our performance if He was willing to sacrifice relationship, but He refuses to do that.

Of course, that's not how we operate. The surest defense of the gospel's truth is simple: a human being would never have come up with it. We are driven by performance. We live in a culture that worships excellence in all of its expressions. We want excellent service at excellent restaurants so we can enjoy excellent conversation with our excellent friends. Excellence is our Holy Grail.

But God, who is the definition of excellence, is primarily in pursuit of our hearts, not our output. That doesn't mean He's unconcerned with His mission—Jesus, after all, "came to set captives free." This mission consumes Him. If Satan, as the Bible tells us, thinks only about how to "kill, steal, and destroy," then God thinks constantly about how to set captives free. He is the headwaters of an archetype that goes deep in us: the superhero who sacrifices everything to save. But this superhero must have His counterpart, just as Batman must have his Robin. That counterpart is you and me, if we will offer Jesus the only thing that is really ours to give.

Our skin in the game.

FOR DISCUSSION OR PERSONAL REFLECTION

- "God wants teammates, not fans." If you took that statement seriously today, how might it challenge the way you live your life?
- In what ways would you say you've invested your skin in the game with God?

NOTES

Introduction

1. The story of Warren Buffet's first use of "skin in the game" is widely reported but also suspect. William Safire, the *New York Times* columnist, claimed to have debunked the story, but he could not track down a definitive genesis for the phrase. What is true is that Buffet's first investment fund was bankrolled by eleven doctors, and he did kick in $100 of his own money.
2. Henry David Thoreau, *Walden and Other Writings* (Red Lion, PA: Empire Books, 2012), 4.
3. Jim Elliot, *The Journals of Jim Elliot* (Grand Rapids: Revell, 1974), 174.

Chapter 1: Will You Face Your Shame?

1. Marianne K. G. Tanabe, "Health and Health Care of Japanese-American Elders," Department of Geriatric Medicine, John A. Burns School of Medicine, University of Hawaii, http://www.stanford.edu/group/ethnoger/japanese.html.
2. Jin Li, Lianqin Wang, and Kurt W. Fischer, "The Organization of Chinese Shame Concepts," *Cognition and Emotion* 18, no. 6 (2004), 767–97.
3. From a lecture by Dr. Allan Schore titled "The Neuropsychology of Attachment." Referenced in Joseph Burgo, "Attachment Theory and the Origins of Shame," *After Psychotherapy* (blog), posted December 10, 2011, http://www.afterpsychotherapy.com/attachment-theory-and-shame.
4. Joseph Burgo, "Attachment Theory and the Origins of Shame," *After*

Psychotherapy (blog), posted December 10, 2011, http://www.afterpsy chotherapy.com/attachment-theory-and-shame.

5. Ibid.

6. Brené Brown, "Listening to Shame," TED.com, March 2012, http://www.ted.com/talks/brene_brown_listening_to_shame.

7. Ibid.

8. Author Jim Collins first coined this phrase in his book *Good to Great: Why Some Companies Make the Leap . . . and Others Don't* (New York: HarperCollins, 2010), 13.

9. Brené Brown, "Listening to Shame."

Chapter 2: Will You Receive Grace?

1. C. S. Lewis, *The Great Divorce* (New York: HarperCollins, 2009), 27–28.

2. Chris Carter and David Duchovny, "Talitha Cumi," *The X-Files*, Season 3, episode 24, directed by R. W. Goodwin, aired May 17, 1996.

3. Barna Group, "Americans Describe Their Views About Life After Death," Barna.org, October 21, 2003, https://www.barna.org/barna-update/5-barna-update/128-americans-describe-their-views-about-life-after-death#.U4tSFNyZnJA.

4. Michka Assayas, *Bono: In Conversation with Michka Assayas* (New York: Penguin, 2005), 225.

5. Edwin Friedman, *A Failure of Nerve: Leadership in the Age of the Quick Fix* (New York: Church, 2007).

6. Sheldon Vanauken, *A Severe Mercy* (New York: HarperCollins, 2009).

Chapter 3: Will You Embrace Your True Identity?

1. From author's notes, taken during a 2009 Comic-Con panel discussion that included Andy Grossberg, editor of *Tripwire Magazine*.

2. Oswald Chambers, "Will You Go Out Without Knowing?" January 2 devotional in *My Utmost For His Highest: An Updated Edition in Today's Language: The Golden Book of Oswald Chambers* (Grand Rapids: Discovery House, 2012).

3. Seth Godin, "The Media Needs a Narrative," Seth's Blog, posted

November 5, 2013, http://sethgodin.typepad.com/seths_blog/2013
/11/the-media-needs-a-narrative.html.

4. C. S. Lewis, *The Silver Chair* (New York: HarperCollins, 2002), 172.

Chapter 4: Will You Own What You Want?

1. Amanda Palmer, "The Art of Asking," TED.com, February 2013,
   https://www.ted.com/talks/amanda_palmer_the_art_of_asking.
2. John Eldredge, *The Journey of Desire* (Nashville: Nelson, 2000), 20.
3. Instilling Goodness School, City of Ten Thousand Buddhas, "Following the Buddha's Footsteps," San Francisco State University, http://
   online.sfsu.edu/rone/Buddhism/footsteps.htm.
4. C. S. Lewis, *The Weight of Glory and Other Addresses* (New York: Macmil-
   lan, 1980), 3–4.
5. William P. Young, interview for a Lifetree Café episode, "Can God
   Love a Mess Like Me?," week of February 12, 2012, http://lifetreecafe
   .com/topics/2012/february/can-god-love-a-mess-like-me/.
6. Feifei Sun, "Are You In a Codependent Relationship," WebMD.com,
   accessed October 6, 2014, http://www.webmd.com/sex-relationships
   /features/signs-of-a-codependent-relationship.

Chapter 5: Will You Confront Your Fears?

1. George MacDonald, *Unspoken Sermons* (Whitefish, MN: Kessinger,
   2010), 106.
2. U.S. Department of Justice, Office of Justice Programs, National
   Institute of Justice, *Youth Victimizations: Prevalence and Implications*,
   by Dean G. Kilpatrick, Benjamin E. Saunders, and Daniel W. Smith.
   NCJ 194972 (Washington D.C., Office of Justice Programs, 2003),
   https://www.ncjrs.gov/pdffiles1/nij/194972.pdf.
3. Alix Spiegel, "Boston Blasts a Reminder of 'The Fragility of Life,'"
   NPR's *Morning Edition*, April 17, 2013, http://www.npr.org/blogs
   /health/2013/04/17/177562770/Boston-Blasts-Remind
   -Us-Of-Fragility-Of-Life.
4. Ibid.

5. Ibid.

6. John Eldredge, in discussion with the author, May 16, 2002.

7. Benjamin Hochman, "No Going Soft in Hardened NFL," *Denver Post*, November 10, 2013, http://www.denverpost.com/hochman /ci_24492068/no-going-soft-hardened-nfl.

8. Horatio G. Spafford, "It Is Well With My Soul," 1873.

9. Ben Giliberti, "It's Not the Box, It's the Bulk," *Washington Post*, July 20, 2005, http://www.washingtonpost.com/wp-dyn/content/article /2005/07/19/AR2005071900312.html.

Chapter 6: Will You Risk?

1. From a list of responses given at a men's retreat sponsored by Greenwood Community Church in the fall of 2012.

Chapter 7: Will You Wait, Even When All Hope Is Lost?

1. "Where Does the Time Go?" Timex Releases Results of Survey Detailing How Americans Spend Their Time," TimexGroup.com, September 25, 2012, http://timexgroup.com/news/press-20120925 -survey-data.html.

2. Alex Stone, "Why Waiting Is Torture," *New York Times* Sunday Review, August 18, 2012, http://www.nytimes.com/2012/08/19/opinion/sun day/why-waiting-in-line-is-torture.html?pagewanted=all&_r=0.

3. Ibid.

4. Ibid.

5. John Ortberg, from a sermon that was later included in a collection of sermons published as a short Kindle book titled *Waiting On God* (Carol Stream, IL: Christianity Today, 2012).

6. From author's notes taken during a lecture given by N. T. Wright at the Simply Jesus Gathering, November 7–9, 2013.

7. Simone Weil, *Waiting for God* (New York: HarperCollins, 2009), 103.

8. "Why Do We Hate Waiting?" Institute for Cognitive Sciences and Technologies, accessed October 6, 2014, http://istc.cnr.it/question /why-do-we-hate-waiting.

9. Edwin Friedman, *A Failure of Nerve: Leadership in the Age of the Quick Fix* (New York: Church, 2007), 33.

10. Ortberg, *Waiting On God.*

11. Weil, *Waiting for God*, 103.

12. Joseph Pearce, *Wisdom and Innocence: A Life of G.K. Chesterton* (San Francisco, CA: Ignatius Press, 1997), 151.

Chapter 8: Will You Make Jesus Your First and Last Resort?

1. Homer, *The Odyssey* (New York: Bloomsbury, 2014), 130.

2. Rosie Shuster et al. "Jaws II," *Saturday Night Live*, season 1, episode 4, directed by Dave Wilson.

3. C. S. Lewis, *The Lion, the Witch and the Wardrobe* (New York: HarperCollins, 1994), 48.

4. Christian Smith and Melinda Lundquist Denton, *Soul Searching: The Religious and Spiritual Lives of American Teenagers* (New York: Oxford University Press, 2009).

5. Ibid.

6. From a personal note from Ned Erickson to the author.

7. Jim Collins, *Good to Great: Why Some Companies Make the Leap . . . and Others Don't* (New York: HarperCollins, 2010), 13.

8. From a personal note from Ned Erickson to the author.

Epilogue

1. Mentioned in Philip Yancey, "Yancey: Chords That Bind," *Christianity Today*, September 1, 1997, http://www.christianitytoday.com /ct/1997/september1/7ta120.html.